The NERD Factor

The Hidden Hindrance
that will
Stall any Software Solution

John Chambers

ISBN-13: 9781089927594

Some illustrations provided by Microsoft ClipArt

This book is dedicated to
those who have had to
suffer the indignity of nerds
everywhere.

And to those who have
suffered the indignity of
being incorrectly labeled
"nerd."

Why we Do what we Do

This book was originally written in 1985. The story of its 35-year journey is told in "What is a Nerd?" below but the important point here is that after formatting the old 1985 text files into some semblance of a publishable book, the manuscript was passed around to a number of professionals currently working in the field.

They were generous with their comments and suggestions and many have been used. Every professional, in one way or another, took this passage in "Programming as an Art" as the reason he or she is in this field:

"I can do that?" the user asks.

"Yes," the software professional says and with the touch of a key, a tap on the screen, a swish of a mouse, the task is done.

"You have made my day!" says the user, and *that* is what a real professional lives for.

Table of Contents

What is a Nerd?

Involved in almost any software project, lurking in the vicinity of nearly every electronic installation, will be found the NERD. A nerd does not necessarily wear eyeglasses held together with adhesive tape, nor is the breast-pocket pen holder his plastic badge. Physical appearance does not a nerd make.

Some people, incorrectly labeled nerds, are technical wizards. Keeping technology humming and productive, useful to those who need reliable information right now, these so-called nerds are valuable assets. Eccentric at times, these folks are not true nerds. The true nerd has been totally captivated by fascinating electronic technology.

Those words were written in 1985. I was making more money than I knew how to spend. An "independent contractor, computer programmer," also lovingly known as a "hired gun," was a lucrative profession.

By writing up my successful actions, I figured, I could get out of that computer business and pursue the life of a "writer" complete with red fez and blue slippers.

It didn't work out that way. But let me start at the beginning ...

In the late 1970s, as the Inventory Manager at a factory, I had barely heard of "computers." My department, along with the rest of the company, began a process known as "getting computerized." The boss bought some package, hardware and software, and a fellow to make it all work.

The fellow could have been called a nerd but a more politely, he "lacked people skills." I saw the disaster he was creating by refusing to make the "computer" do what was needed. And he was making 25 bucks an hour, a princely sum in the late '70s.

It was apparent I could clean up if I learned about computers and perhaps become a go-between, between people who needed "computerization" and those who could make the computers sing. Long before RadioShack marketed their "TRS-80" and way before Microsoft was a household word, I read books, made up exercises, and taught myself how to program using a dinky "AlphaMicro" owned by a friend. He wanted to track Commodities quotes and predict Futures based on his own algorithms. I made it do just what he wanted. He never told me if he made money with it or not.

I learned enough about loops and goto's to take myself around to local software shops, knock on doors and announce, "I are a programmer." One of them hired me at minimum wage – like 3 bucks an hour as I recall – with the promise that if I did well, I would get raises. Within six months, I was making 25 bucks an hour and was the company's go-to guy for designing software systems for their clients.

A falling out of the principals left me with no job but also a number of clients with no one to make their data make sense. Within a couple of years I had lucrative contracts and a crew of programmers. I think they are called "custom software engineers" these days. Some were Nerds, some were not.

Any manager who is going to hire or deal with a software project needs to have a basic understanding of software. In the same way the driver of a car does not need to know the nuances of carburetion versus fuel injection, a project manager only needs to know what the steering wheel does and how to step on the accelerator and the brake. As a manager, you do not need to know the bits and bytes, but you do need to know what analysis is, what a design should look like and how to test.

This is not a technical manual on the latest whiz-bang technology. If it were, it would be out of date the moment you bought it. A number of manuals and basic books, tutorials and informal expositions, are available on line or any place good books gather. This book will add nothing to that library.

This is not even a book on how to manage a project. It is a book on what to look for and how to handle the people involved in the project.

The technical publishers of 1985 were not interested in my little offering and regular publishers feared it would be too technical.

My dreams of a red fez and blue slippers went on the shelf and I built a little client base, thinking I was going to get out of this business any minute.

Thirty years later, 2015 almost to the day, I helped my last client transition over to more modern technology and retired from that life. I write on other subjects but never did look good in a red fez.

In late 2018, I mentioned this unpublished manuscript to Lindsay Bassett, a high-powered software consultant. She related that she had been looking for a book exactly like this and encouraged me to dust it off.

All that remained of the book was one faded hard-copy manuscript and a set of text files saved from my old Radio Shack "Trash-80."

As I formatted and edited these text files into the book you are reading, Lindsay read these words just to make sure I did not date it too much. When I talked about buggy-whips, Lindsay suggested a more modern example.

It would be a major goof if I also did not mention Viken Nokhoudian, a phone app developer, his latest entrepreneurial endeavor, was also generous in his suggestions – and his location of typos.

The Musack Brothers, Scott and Paul, my step-sons, also perused this book. As had I, each had taught himself about computers and programming. One is the main programmer for a health and nutrition company. The other is a Senior Systems Administrator for a government agency. Each is very familiar with nerds, especially those surrounded by government employees. Their comments were well-taken.

The Nerd Factor has been around since the beginning of history. From the Greeks, to the Hebrews, to the abacus and the earliest days of the Jacquard loom, from ENIAC to blockchain programming, human nature stays the same. A nerd programming a 19th century jacquard loom is going to produce unusable cloth and *that* is a software disaster!

Beyond eccentric, the true nerd can devastate a software project by rudely neglecting other people. Because technology is interesting, one must be wary of the bewitching qualities of new technology. One must watch for the Nerd factor in oneself and in others.

The Nerd Factor is, as portrayed in the Microsoft ClipArt illustration on the next page, the intersection of Intelligence, Obsession and Social Ineptitude.

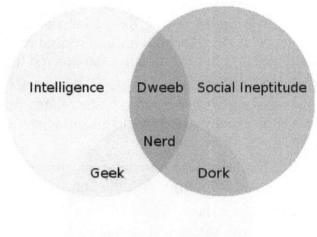

Many factors go into the completion of a software project. The Nerd factor is the deadliest. In any programming effort, barring power failures and Acts of God, any cost or time over-run can be traced to this factor. It can creep into any stage of the project and kill it dead as a hammer.

Software projects are notorious for running longer and costing more than they should. The Nerd factor is an epidemic. The Nerd factor, however, is not a disease: it is only a symptom. The causes of the malady must be known to cure the symptom and save the project. To complete your project on-time and on-budget, the Nerd factor must be overcome.

It can be.

John Chambers
December 2018

Chapter 1: PROFESSIONAL FLAKES

A client once told me, "All computer programmers are flakes – but you're ok." What he meant was that other technology professionals in his experience were either

a) unreliable,
b) too expensive,
c) arrogant,
d) unprofessional, or
e) all of the above.

He was only expressing the frustration felt by thousands of Information Technology project managers. IT projects are notorious for cost overruns and never getting done.

That only *appears* to be the source of frustration. All too often, computer professionals are wrapped up in jargon and electronic details. The business manager / owner whose livelihood depends on computerization must either rely on a flakey priest-of-electronics or fire him, hoping the next consultant he hires will be less alien. Either choice can be expensive and nerve shattering.

OR the manager can learn to tell the difference between the "flake" and the professional. That is what this book is about. It contains the "how-tos" to complete a computer project on-time, on-budget.

Reading Computer Books

Anyone paying for or managing a software project needs to have a basic understanding of software and how to manage any project. This book gives you a little of that assuming the reader has zero experience. If you already have some familiarity with software and management tools, it will be a basic review.

You will want to read more. To deal with the nerd factor, do not bother with technical books. A highly-recommended book for managers in 1980 describing how to computerize a small business very carefully showed pictures of different types of equipment. Punched computer cards and the operation of a keypunch machine (used for punching the cards) are described and illustrated. No computer professional worth his salt would dream of advising the use of a keypunch. After five years, that portion of the book was archaic at best. Any book will be out-dated to the degree that it promotes the fallacy that "computerization" has to do with machinery. Certainly the machine, also called "hardware" or "iron," is necessary for computerization, but businesses are coming to learn that the iron, once in place, is of minimal importance.

Another book, written in 1979, dealt with some of the methods to employ in the quest for the perfect system. Although hardware is hardly mentioned, computerization seems to take place mystically on some remote planet. That technical manual was written to improve the specialized skill of an already competent computer professional. For the most part, it will never go out of date, although some of the examples will become laughable. "Oh, yes," the computer expert of tomorrow will say goodnaturedly, "I remember we used to have that sort of problem, before the Whizzle-Bang system came out – how primitive!" To the business person, whose business and very life depend on the proper and effective use of a compter system, technical manuals similar to those described above are useless.

This book you are reading is devoted to eradicating the "nerd factor" in computer projects thus allowing them to be completed on-time and on-budget. It does not pretend to reveal the fine tricks of programming. Businesses hire computer professionals to bring their computer dreams to reality and take care of all the gritty details of making the machine work. This book you are about to read does not delve into the dirty trifles of programming the perfect system.

Although this book is its own kind of technical manual, it will not tell the reader how to become a "worker" in the computer field. Certainly "workers" are needed: brilliant people graduate from the computer sciences department of one or another "Acme Technical School" and are hired by any one of a number of banks, insurance companies, government agencies or giant manufacturers. Working each day on the 37th floor of any of a number of tall buildings in the downtown of any of a number of cities, the work is less than exciting, but all medical and dental needs are covered. This book is not an employment agency. It is not a technical manual on how to become a "worker," but I think many "workers" will discover that they can become professionals rather than just another rat in the race.

In all, this is a technical manual. It describes the activities and techniques used by a computer *professional*. For the business owner or manager, it will show the difference between the professional and the flake. It is a yardstick to determine if the person he is about to hire is going to do the job or not.

Smaller is Better

In the same way that businesses are discovering they operate more efficiently by considering themselves an aligned collection of smaller units rather than a faceless monolith, a programmer or project leader for a LARGE concern finds that most of his time is occupied in handling the demands of smaller units within the larger business. In that sense, anyone who thinks himself or herself a "worker" for BIG business is actually a "professional for smaller businesses."

This is a technical manual on how to be a reliable programmer-analyst-consultant, the go-to information technology expert, for a smaller business. For the business person faced with the prospect of hiring a computer whiz, it is a manual on how to recognize the computer professional, thus avoiding costly nerd-like mistakes. This is a manual on how to realize the quest for a reliable system.

It has been estimated that at least half of the cost of a computer system is in the additional programming required to get the machine to do *exactly* what the business needed in the first place. If three sets of programmers have to be hired and fired before finally finding the ones who actually make a system that is reliable, the cost of the system has sky-rocketed beyond tolerance. More than one business, I have been told, has thrown out the computer entirely for exactly this reason.

As a successful programmer, analyst, and consultant for many smaller businesses (and smaller divisions of very large businesses), and having dealt with many business-people and programmers and analysts and consultants over the years, it has become apparent that technical genius is not a guarantee of success in a computer enterprise. There are many computer professionals who are technical wizards, but who, I have been told, are "flakes."

This technical manual describes the reliable computer professional, and how to avoid the pitfalls of being a "worker" or a "flake."

The difficulty with "flakey" computer professionals is that they may be technically proficient, but lack a sense of good business. One consultant quiped that being in business for himself had taught him Integrity and Wisdom. Integrity, he said, was "keeping your promises." Wisdom, however, was "not promising anything." The true nerd is not aware that integrity and wisdom are necessary. However witty the definitions, it is necessary in business to make promises – and keep them.

This is a technical manual on the business of making computers do *exactly* what smaller businesses need and want them to do. Some portions of this book deal exclusively with information needed by the "independent contractor" computer consultant to make his consulting business *very* successful. The entire book, however, comprises those actions and attitudes necessary to get and keep a computer system operational. Whether the system tracks the inventory for a mom-and-pop wholesaler or manages the finances of a multi-national financial institution which must meet the requirements of multiplied divisions on numerous continents, the computer system must be reliable for the individual "users."

Workers, snug on the 37th floor, may never see a user. In their drudgery, workers make mistakes. Nerds are impassioned with the marvels of modern electronics. In their electronic intensity, nerds deliver wonderful systems that don't do what the user wanted. Letting a worker or a nerd loose on a system on which the user depends can be catastrophic. Nothing can be quite as heartbreaking and frustrating as spending gross sums for a system that doesn't work. Firing workers and legal action against nerds may be pleasant revenge, but it still doesn't make the system do what was intended. Only a reliable professional can do that.

For the competent professional, nothing can be quite as satisfying as a system that gets the job done. This is a manual on how to satisfy users. Every user is his own "small business," whether Mom-and-Pop or the Vice-President of the Biscuit Division of Multi-National Food, Inc.

A Word for Independent Contractors

Working with smaller businesses (the mom-and-pop variety) is not only the easiest computer field to break into, it is, in my opinion, one of the most valuable services a computer professional can perform.

In the "What is a Nerd?" introduction, I describe how I got into this business. At the start, after reading a few books and working on a little machine owned by a friend, I went out and showed I could do the job. Within a year or two my independent business had a number of clients and my fees were at the local survey average.

The importance of service to a "small business" has, I think, a special reward not found in working exclusively for mega-sized concerns.

The courage of the small business-person, who independently decides to carve out a niche in the economy by providing a product better than his or her competitors, has been the bedrock of the economy of every civilization worthy of its name. The artisans, farmers, craftworkers, and tradesmen from ancient times to the present have been the foundation on which thriving economies have flourished.

Ancient China's riches did not come from China-Cola, Inc., but from the shrewdness of her traders. No matter where one went in the Far East, to the top of the most rugged mountain, or the center of the densest jungle, one would find a hut in a clearing, bearing the proud legend "Mom and Pop Wu's Trading Post: Browsers Welcome."

Rome may have conquered with her legions, but they only paved the way for the hordes of potters and weavers hawking their goods to war-torn housewives.

England, that "little island of shopkeepers," grew to hold an Empire that spanned the globe. Her power rested as much in her shopkeepers as it was in her naval strength.

The yeoman farmers in Virginia's hinterland and the silversmiths and tea merchants of Boston started their own nation, under God, and the United States of America came into being. Shopkeepers, blacksmiths, and gold hunters spread the new country across a continent, and the USA became a world power.

Some will argue that there are other factors involved, military might, strategic position, natural resources, etc., and certainly these are factors – but it has been the "small businessmen" who supply the economic energy on which armies march and civilizations survive. In terms of keeping a civilization alive, there can be no more effective action than helping the smaller businessman keep his head above water.

In the current age of huge businesses dispensing one-size-fits-all products to entire populations and huge governments promulgating impersonal regulations on one and all, it has become difficult for the smaller businessman to compete. The first computers, monster machines filling entire city blocks and requiring the waters of Niagra to cool them, could only be afforded by huge impersonal enterprises. Government agencies and multi-national corporations bought them. It might be said that these new machines perfectly fit the image of these businesses, both public and private. Big businesses could calculate, regulate, and keep their records at the speed of light. Smaller businesses looked doomed.

Then came smaller, less expensive computers. More small businesses started to buy them. Keeping his head above water, the modern smaller businessman, the backbone of the economy of *any* civilization, will use his computer to its maximum efficiency. With a resurgence of the economic base, I think it not too adventurous to say that we are looking at the beginnings of a new civilization.

Computers will not solve all the problems of the civilization, but a thriving economy with maximum employment has higher morale than the depression-ridden masses of the oppressed and unemployed. Less crime, too. Statistically, smaller businesses employ more workers than the huge impersonal ones. Our modern artisans, craftspeople, and traders must be allowed to flourish and prosper. Their efficient use of computers will help them do that.

But with running a business and coping with competition, what businessman will have time to learn how to get his computer to do the best it can for him? Who can be hired to handle this?

The Computer Professional

In the early days of computers, the computer professional worked on the 37th floor of an impersonal building. One was expected to perform his own assembly-line task. In some places, curiosity about areas not under one's immediate purview was (and is) actively discouraged. The programmer is not required to know how the system will be used. He is only expected to "work." The Information Systems Department may have hundreds of personnel.

In the smaller business, the professional is expected to be knowledgeable in many – if not all – aspects of the system. For a smaller business, the professional may discover, to his dismay, that he *is* Information Systems.

Computers are here to stay. People will always be needed to keep them humming and responsive to the demands placed on them. As technology advances, the day to day activity of the computer professional will change. The daily schedule of the consultant for a mom-and-pop store-front will be different than the activities of a programmer for a department of a division of a galaxy-wide concern. But whatever the work-a-day tasks of the future might be, the purpose of the computer professional will be the same – making systems that work on-time and on-budget, and keeping them operational. Nerds cannot do it, only professionals will do.

Chapter 2: COMPUTERIZATION IS NECESSARY

The sign boasted "*SUDDEN* Service."

In this fast-paced age of overnight deliveries and instant food, a business cannot expect to survive without rapid service. Customers have come to rely on instant gratification – although perhaps not suddenly. Their needs can be rapidly transmitted and processed with the aid of a computer. Because computerization has invaded almost every industry, it could be said that the business without a computer will be left behind, even if only in the area of customer service. People enjoy having their desires fulfilled immediately. Given the choice between placing an order and having it delivered in an hour or sometime next week, other circumstances being equal, most folks will opt for delivery today.

For a company to grow, it must also be able to handle more transactions than it did previously. A computer is eminently qualified to process vast quantities of transactions without complaining of overwork or demanding a vacation. Processing orders and invoices and the mountain of paperwork associated with a thriving concern is, in essence, a series of simple actions strung together. Because a computer is programmed by stringing together a series of simple instructions, like pearls on a string, it can be seen that a computer is the obvious solution to the simple, repetitive actions of the day-to-day flow of business.

As the mundane chores of processing the flows of business become handled by the computer, this flow can increase without undue strain on employees. The employees who deal with customers, vendors and the myriad contacts of any business are not bogged down in swamps of paper and can devote more personal attention to their contacts. Not only is service speedier with a computer, it can and should be perceived as more personal. The great cry that was once heard about computers "depersonalizing" business does not have to exist. It certainly is incorrect to blame a piece of electronic gadgetry for surly salesmen.

Any business, however well-managed, comes to a time when a change is needed. A sudden overstock in widgits will indicate to the astute manager that "business as usual" will no longer carry the day for the Widgit Division. Without a reliable data system in a fast-paced world, managers and owners will not discover the problems their companies face until those problems have become crises. Computers can be programmed to report on possible problems before they become crises.

When a problem is spotted, a change is needed. The alert owner or manager suddenly has to answer questions: "Should we be selling more widgits?" or "Do we need to open an office in Timbuktu?" It is time for a decision.

Making a Decision

To make the right choice about widgits or Timbuktu, a manager needs correct data – rapidly. If widgits sales are to be expanded, the decision needs to be made right now, before the market shifts and they go out of style or the competition finds a way to make them cheaper. If that office on another continent is to be opened, plans must be laid, starting right now, before the territory is saturated with someone else's widgits.

The data to be considered will include observations that are not stored in the computer, of course. A sudden overstock in widgits coupled with the off-hand remark from a customer, "My brother lives in Timbuktu, and sure likes your widgits," and the brochure from the City Council of Timbuktu promising lower taxes, and the "unofficial leak" that widgits do or do not cause blindness in mice, and a dozen other indicators from the environment are sifted to produce alternative futures for the business.

The astute manager will, at this point, turn to the data within his company to make his decision. "How many widgits *do* we have?" and "How fast do we sell them?" and "Which of our salesmen pushes the most of them?" and "Have we sold any in Timbuktu?" are questions that can be answered by a reliable computer system. Based on the answers to these questions a sound business decision can be made.

Even the relatively simple daily decision: "Do we make a loan to this entity?" is, and should be, based on electronic data. Although it has been a long-standing policy (in 1985) for a certain un-named bank to require projected balance sheets to accompany substantial loan applications, I have been told that that policy was not enforced when those projected financial statements had to be done by hand. It is small wonder to me that lending institutions made a number of bad loans during that period. With the advent of easy-to-use spread-sheet programs, I understand, this policy is again being enforced. Hopefully, there will be fewer bad loans.

(By 2018, after years of Government diddling in the loan markets, more attention is paid to "what will the regulators say?" than many other business practices.)

Business decisions, whether making loans, opening an office on another continent, or slowing down widgit production, should be based on accurate and timely data. When the data is lacking, choices are chancy.

Without a reliable system (which means reliable software), the gathering of the data can be either accurate or timely, but rarely both. Sometimes, as in the case of the loans described above, the data is skipped altogether. What makes the data so difficult to compile is that file cabinets have to be emptied and mountains of papers gone through and sorted and sifted and added up. The individual tasks of sorting and sifting and adding are not difficult, but it is the sheer volume that makes the data-gathering process so difficult. Luckily, a computer can do the sorting and sifting and adding up at the speed of light.

It could be said that 80 per cent of the work involved in making a decision is in the compiling of the data. Twenty per cent is in the formulation of alternatives and making the choice. That 80 per cent of the job is dull-eyed drudgery. Software exists to do the deadening part of the task.

The Pareto Theory

The Pareto theory, also known as the 80/20 rule, is well-known in inventory management. While an inventory may include thousands of items, it has been found that only a small number of those items provide a large portion of income. For instance, in an inventory of 1,000 different styles and colors of gaskets and widgits, it will be found that the top-selling 10 items account for 25 per cent of the company's revenue. The lower 500 items might account for only 5 per cent. A very few items from the top of the list produce a large majority of the income while the large majority of items produce only a small portion of sales.

The general consensus is that 20 per cent of the inventory produces 80 per cent of sales, and 80 per cent of the inventory produces only 20 per cent of the sales. Similarly, 80% of your complaints come from 20% of your customers.

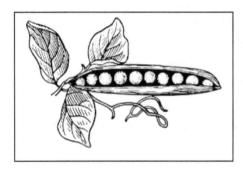

The original observation by Vilfredo Pareto that 20% of the pea plants in his garden produced 80% of the peas was the start of what has become known as the Pareto Theory or the 80/20 principle. You get the idea: 80% of the results come from 20% of the possible causes.

Extending Pareto's theory to decision-making and tasks in general, it can be seen that 80 per cent of a task is low-yield toil while 20 per cent is high-yield creative activity that actually produces a decision or a product.

In sales, 80 per cent of the job is taken up in homework and ground work and cold calls and flat refusals. The other 20 per cent of the job is in making the pitch and handling the objections and ending up with a name on the dotted line. In writing a report (or a book!), 80 per cent of the job is in collecting the data and sifting it and sorting it and then laboriously putting words on paper. The other 20 per cent is in seeing what the report needs to convey and what data to present to have the report make sense.

Eighty per cent of any task is dull-eyed mechanical activity which supports the 20 per cent that actually gets the job done. The 80 per cent is necessary to do, it cannot be skipped, but it is work that a person of lesser ability could do mechanically rather than tying up a person of higher ability with mundane details.

Organizationally, the truth of this can be seen in any enterprise. For instance, high-powered lawyers and even judges have researchers and clerks to do the mundane tasks involved in writing briefs and legal decisions. The boss of a company has a secretary to open the mail and take telephone calls. The secretary has a receptionist. The receptionist has phone.

A sales organization has its salesmen and then it has prospectors to qualify possible customers and a word processor to draw up the contracts. Put bluntly, it has been said that 80 per cent of a job could be done by anyone while the reason *you* have your position is because *you* bring a special 20 per cent of attitude and experience and professionalism. Without the unique qualities that you bring to your job, 80 per cent of it could be done by your next door neighbor.

An analysis of the American steel industry has even been done based on the Pareto theory. Most of the American steel industry, the analysis goes, is losing ground, because basic steel products (80 per cent of the steel market) can be and are being produced in third-world countries where heavy industry is just starting to come into its own. Basic steel products can be produced by "anyone," so those American companies that are trying to make these products are losing out to the less-skilled labor that floods other countries and produces less expensive basic steel. American steel giants are losing their grip on the market. On the other hand, those American companies that produce fine alloy steel products, steel that requires more skill to produce (20 per cent of the market) find they have no competition. According to that analysis, the American steel industry's market has shifted. Those companies who are still trying to do the 80 per cent that "anyone" can do are the ones who are hurting.

The reason you have *your* position is for the 20 per cent that you bring to it. The other 80 per cent of your job could be done mechanically. The way for you to enhance your position would be to expand the 20 per cent. To do that, the 80 per cent has to be minimized.

The only reason you need a reliable computer system is to minimize the 80 per cent, so you can increase that 20 per cent contribution that makes that job *yours*.

The Four Parts of any System

Traditionally, the "four parts" of a computer are the memory, the processor, inputs and outputs. Those are chunks of intricate metal and glass, but they are not a *system*.

The "four parts" we're talking about have broader application than software or computers. They have to do with any system devised by Humans. Computers or software provide an excellent example of a "system" but the four parts apply equally to driving a car, doing dinner dishes or setting up a government.

The first part of any system, let's use computers as an example, is the most important part. It is frequently overlooked. No system has any value – I mean none at all – without this most essential element.

The most important part of the system is the USER. This part of the system is called, by professionals in the know, "U." Without "U," the system has no reason for being.

The purpose of the system is to minimize the 80 per cent of your job that is drudgery so "U" can expand into the more creative aspects of your work. The system is there to serve you, and you should remember that the next time someone tells you that computers are so-o-o complex and take years of study. (Same for driving a car or designing a government, by the way.)

If the system isn't minimizing the drudgery of your job, if it is too difficult to work with, if it is just downright unfriendly, it is because some whiz-kid hasn't been clever enough to make the machine work for "U."

The most obvious part of a computer system is you. But that is so obvious, it tends to be overlooked.

The next most obvious part of a computer is the physical machine itself. This is usually boxes of metal. In 1985, some looked like washing machines and others look like TVs and typewriters. Today they are tiny laptops, surfaces or simply a "phone." Next year, who knows?

Inside the old washing machines or modern phones are shards of silicon (called chips) and miles of connections. This stuff is called HARDWARE. It is also called "iron." Iron is needed to make a computer system, but it is not the system itself – no more than canvas and pigments make a great painting or a chunk of metal makes an automobile. Iron can be fascinating, and some computer buffs spend years fiddling around with all this and sometimes end up speaking what seems to be a foreign language. The language is hardware-ese, but don't let it throw you. Remember that all that fancy talk about "bits" and "bytes" and "RAM" and "ROM" are not as important to the system as you, the user.

Once the iron is in place, it has to be turned into a system. The dictionary says a system is a number of "interrelated" parts. All the wires and RAM and touch-screens and rig-a-ma-rol, all the iron, sits there, not yet interrelated. To get all these pieces of machinery to work together requires what is called SYSTEM SOFTWARE. The system software is the third part of a computer. It turns a heap of iron into a system.

It is as though there were a pile of gears and wheels and spark plugs and thing-a-ma-bobs on the garage floor. That is the iron. A mechanic comes along and puts all the pieces together. The pile of iron has become recognizable as an automobile, but it still is not a usable "system." Add some gas and turn the key and the heap of iron coughs into life, purrs, and becomes a carriage ready to be driven. That is what system software does for the computer, turning it into an affair ready to be driven.

The fourth part of a computer system is the instructions fed to the system that tell it where to go. A car sitting in the garage is of no use. To be of value, it needs to be driven somewhere. The car needs to be instructed by appropriate application of throttle, brake and steering. In a computer system, these instructions are called APPLICATIONS or APPLICATION SOFTWARE, lately shortened to APPS. To be of value, the system needs to be applied to a task, in the same way a car needs to be driven. You have to add apps to make it worthwhile.

Application software is the throttle and steering wheel and brake used to drive the system to the user's destination. When a system is described as easy to use or "friendly" – or difficult to use and unfriendly, it is the apps being described. If a system is "unfriendly,"

it would be like saying that an automobile is difficult to drive – because the steering wheel is in the back seat or the brake pedal is on the roof. When users (or potential users) hire a computer consultant, they should have only a passing interest in the hardware or system software. Interest in the iron and system software should be confined to cost and assurance that it will be adequately supported.

The wise consultant will recognize the importance of the user, seeing him or her as *the* essential ingredient to the system. Assisting users to make their jobs easier is where the computer professional's attention should be – rather than on the machine or system software. As far as the user is concerned, the machine and system software are invisible. It is the job of the programmer or consultant to keep them that way.

As the technology of hardware and the efficiency of system software advances, how the programmer or consultant does this job will change, but the task itself will remain the same. The role the consultant or programmer plays will be different, but the product of his work will not shift an inch.

The computer professional's calling is to minimize the 80 per cent drudgery so the user can revel in the 20 per cent joy of his or her job. Nerds do not have such a calling. Costly mistakes are the result.

Chapter 3: MILLION DOLLAR MISTAKES

The most important part of a computer is the user. Whether the project is gargantuan or modest in size, whether it is an original installation or modifying an existing system, the system must serve the needs of the user. That is the art of computerization. Any system that does not adhere to the principles of the art of computerization will be an expensive mistake.

How Big Mistakes are Made

In a mega-sized environment, the computer professional finds himself a part of a team. As one of a number of analysts, designers, data-base experts, programmers, technical writers, and user trainers under a hierarchy of project leaders, managers, approvers and counter-signers, the computer professional can be viewed as, and frequently *is* viewed as, a cog in a machine. Plugging away on the 37th floor of the "office," the professional may have job security but the price can be a stifled responsibility.

A quick look will demonstrate how this can cause expensive mistakes. Take the example of a programmer given the specifications ("specs") of a program. The program is expected to be written as laid out in the specs, as it should be. If the specs don't make sense, the programmer will go to the project manager who will get with analysis unit and they'll all go over to the data design team. At some point, one can assume, someone will ask the user.

If the head of one or another department is out of town that week, the program is shelved until later. Later, someone else picks up the specs and can't figure them out either. The journey through channels begins again. Finally the meeting is held. Whether or not the programmer comes away from his meeting understanding how the program fits in the rest of the system, it will be written as specified. The professional, in the computer field or any other, is rightfully expected to do a workmanlike job whether it makes sense or not.

Though expert in his own area, able to consistently turn in well-crafted programs, the example programmer is subject to the failings of the weakest member of his team. The specifications, for example, say that the program is to invoice customers for the widgets they have ordered. Additionally, the cost of the widgets sold is to be added to the cost-of-sales and subtracted from the value-of-inventory. This is a straight-forward spec but the well-crafted program is going to be a costly mistake.

The analyst did not discover from the user that sometimes an invoice has to be written for widgets that have not been counted as stock-on-hand. The system designer did not realize that widgets cannot be considered stock-on-hand until the supplier's bill has been processed. The supplier may not send a timely bill. The data designer and specification writer were totally unaware that the invoicing program will have to be able to ship widgets that "are not there." The programmers write 84 programs based on faulty assumptions.

The user is trained on the system and starts to use it. All goes along well until the first invoice must be written against widgets from a late-billing supplier. The invoicing program backs up and refuses to jump into the land of mythical widgets. "Sorry," it says, "That item cannot be invoiced."

Billing comes to a screeching halt. The user frantically calls IT. Finding no immediate relief, the old, half-forgotten billing system is pressed into service. The Boss pulls his hair out.

Analysts, designers, and programmers down buckets of coffee during weeks of sleepless nights trying to straighten out the frantic complaints that "the system won't let us do our billing!" Millions of dollars of late billings are whipped out by ragged users. Eighty-four torn-up and re-patched programs later, a system that was estimated to cost $200,000 is now closer to a half-million, not counting lost business, war-torn clerks and accounting personnel.

The revised system is installed and the users gingerly try it. This time, the billing rolls out against widgets that "are not there," but the reports on cost-of-sales and value-of-inventory cannot be made to balance. The specifications merely said to add or subtract the "cost" of the widgets, but when shipping mythical widgets, does that mean the last cost or the standard cost or the average cost or no cost? Some programs use one cost and others make adjustments based on something else. The Accounting Department is in an uproar. The CIO is seen stalking the halls muttering to herself. Project managers begin to wear a hunted look. After more heroics from the project team, the bugs are worked out, past data repaired, reports corrected, and the cost of the system is touching the million dollar mark. A year later, it still has bugs – not many – and the project manager has gone to greener pastures.

Cost over-runs, mistakes and failures in a larger environment are not easily traceable to the incompetence of one programmer, manager or person. The problems facing a larger system are *team* failures. Team failures boil down to failures in communication. The competent programmer, part of the team, does a workmanlike job, but he is only as good as the weakest link in his team.

The First Link

The first link is between user and analyst. If the user did not clearly communicate to the analyst what was needed, or overlooked a minor detail (such as the fact that some suppliers bill late), or was not informed what the system could do and therefore was unable to relate what was needed, this link can be very weak indeed.

Although it is the analyst's job to find out what the user wants, users sometimes appear to delight in being difficult. It is the user's responsibility to relate his or her needs to the analyst. Sometimes analysts complain that a particular user is unduly recalcitrant. Occasionally, one or another user will be hiding something, but mostly it is that the user knows his job so well, he does not think about it. As he looks at it, he discovers stuff he knew about but didn't mention because it was not important – did not *seem* important. The late-billing vendor is not something he thinks about. He'll only notice it when it happens and then he'll tell this little tidbit to the analyst.

"Some vendors bill late."

The analyst, who had everything planned out, suddenly has to go back and make sure we can invoice against non-existent inventory – oh, @#&$, that changes everything. Opens a can of worms. But better now than two months later.

It is the analyst's responsibility to discover what the user needs. Sometimes a tight-lipped user has to be coaxed and trained to reveal the system requirements.

Recently, I came across an example of a user who had been *trained* by some computer "expert" to *not* communicate her needs.

The user, Miss T., needed changes to her system so her department could be more productive. In a series of meetings, Miss T. tried to tell me what was needed but with severe hesitations and uncertainties. Her speech was liberally sprinkled with phrases like "I don't know if I'm using the right terminology" and "does that make sense?" It was like dancing with an unwilling bear – very difficult. Although she did not mean to be, she was a user who was "unduly recalcitrant." I thought I saw the source of the problem. Out of the blue, I asked her:

"Has anyone thrown jargon at you and made you feel you don't know what you are talking about?"

"Why, yes!" she exclaimed, and proceeded to tell me about an earlier nerd who had barraged her with unnecessary technical lingo. With that out of the way, Miss T. related exactly what her department needed with great certainty. Within an hour, I had all I needed. The changes she requested were made and came out perfect, first time.

This example is not to say that one must be very careful about "throwing around jargon." The point is that understandable communication delivered with certainty is necessary to the successful completion of any project.

The first link does not require great technical genius. It does require people who are willing to *ask* honest straight forward questions and *listen* to the user's answers.

Other Links

When the analyst communicates his findings to the system design group, his write-up may not be as well organized as it should. It may be difficult for the design group to see the full depth of one or another detail. The analyst may quite clearly relate that "suppliers sometimes bill late," but only a mind-reader would understand the importance of that statement. If the design team does have a swami of remarkable powers and does account for shipments of mythical widgets, this minor facet of the system might become buried in the morass of other details. The program specifications drawn from the design may make only scant mention of late-arriving widgets. The problems of late-billing suppliers may get completely lost in the shuffle.

In workmanlike fashion, the system may be crafted with care, but because earlier links in the chain were weak, it "won't work." Due to earlier communication failures, the programs may not do what the *user* intended, though they could well do what the analyst, what the designer, what the programmer expected.

The cost of the system grows beyond tolerable limits. The project is scrapped. Half the Data Processing Department is fired or quits.

The technical competence of each individual computer professional need not be questioned. Each could be expected to make the computer jump through hoops. The individual computer professional, as a cog in the machine, is unable to take responsibility for more than his small cubicle and hopes that his assignment will somehow fit into the whole. Although some of the individuals on the team will be less competent than they should, and should be fired, the failures of large software projects come from failures to maintain full understandable communication between users, analysts, designers, programmers, documenters, trainers and the rest of the

team. Taking this a step further, even individual incompetence is a failure to train properly and training is very much a matter of communication.

Team performance is a matter of each individual team member being able to listen to and tell others the needs of the users. Technical skill is the ability to translate ideas and actions into something the computer can do. Many people can acquire technical skill – even nerds. Team performance, however, is what will get computer projects completed on time and on budget.

Million dollar mistakes come from team failures. Team failures come from unsuccessful communication. Team performance is an acquired skill, as in the case of Miss T. above. For those who recognize communication as the solution to their system problems, you or members of your staff should look into the work of L. Ron Hubbard on the subject and particularly the "Success through Communication" workshop offered in many major cities.

In a Smaller Environment

Up to this point, attention has been focused on costly errors in larger environments. On a smaller system, whether it is in a department of a larger firm or a store-front operation, the computer professional is still expected to translate user needs into machine operations. The computer professional has to walk the same route as on a larger system, but different shoes have to be worn in the smaller shop.

As in the larger environment, technical skill alone does not guarantee success. Whereas communication is required for team success in the larger shop, it is doubly important in the smaller environment. A technical genius may be able to make the computer sit up and sing, but computer professionals are not paid to "program the computer." The computer professional's pay comes from enabling the user to do something faster or better than could be done previously. In a larger environment, the *team* is expected to produce these new abilities. In a smaller shop, the lone consultant frequently finds that he or she *is* the team.

Being the entire team has its benefits as well as its drawbacks. There is a certain relief in not having to submit to the tyranny of innumerable meetings and "going through channels." Being hired to get the job done in whatever way seems fit can also puff up one's chest. After wallowing in the ecstasy of being one's own boss, the subtle truth, however, will sink in.

The lone consultant finds him- or herself *totally* responsible for the reliability of the entire system. He or she has to be in better than excellent communication with the client or user. The business does not have the budget to import hordes of experts to handle all the details. Any *team* failure, any slight slip in communication, lands squarely on the shoulders of the lone hired gun. In a larger environment, the competence (or incompetence) of individual members of the team is masked by team miscommunication. In the smaller shop, the professional has no shield. If there is a miscommunication, it calls the competence of the consultant into question. The hired gun may or may not be highly technically skilled, but he or she *must* be an expert at communicating. This does not mean being able to swap local gossip. It means being able to listen to users and exactly understand what is being said. It means being able to relate technical details to users without sounding technical. It is an acquired skill. It is a skill not easily mastered.

One place it becomes ultimately important is in areas in which the consultant is not a technical wizard. Bluster and "PR" will never take the place of technical skill because the single hired gun is still ultimately responsible for the reliability of the system.

For example, I am not an expert in electronics. To me, one end of a piece of hardware looks pretty much like another. But the details of hardware maintenance must still be cared for. If one of my clients calls me with a problem, it is my job to solve it. If hardware failure is the source of the difficulty, I have to see that it is righted. I have a "team" in place, so the client only needs to talk to me.

Sometime before this problem came up, I will have told the client that I am ill-equipped to handle hardware problems. I will insist that they put their machine under a "maintenance contract." This usually is not difficult. The machine was originally under warranty from the manufacturer. After the warranty ran out, the manufacturer will contract to continue maintenance for a reasonable fee. There are also numerous "third-party" outfits that will take on hardware maintenance contracts. Once the contract is in place, and I find a problem is linked to the hardware, I'll tell the client to get the hardware people to do their jobs – or I'll make the call to the maintenance firm myself. By communicating,

- first by declaring my limitations to the client – I don't do hardware,
- second by insisting a solution be taken – put hardware maintenance under contract,
- next by letting the client know a particular problem is related to the hardware and
- finally by seeing that the hardware folks do their job,

the area of my incompetence is covered.

The professional, hired to create and modify and maintain a reliable system in a smaller environment, may be quite competent in programming computers, but he or she is in even more danger of tumbling into the same pits that pock the road to a reliable system in a larger shop. It cannot be stressed enough that communication, honest questions, full answers, complete understanding, paves the way to the fulfillment of any computerization project.

There are a few widely-held misconceptions about computerization projects, however, that will kill even the best communication faster than a virus. A couple of the more virulent germs of misconception are discussed below.

Original Creation versus Evolution

This is not a discussion of the nature of God, but describes how a software system comes into being. When a new user first hears that a system is to be installed, he or she will not be certain what abilities the system will give. The user may not be able to articulate what would be desirable. Even if the user is thoroughly familiar with the business functions to be programmed, it is unlikely that every detail will be able to be related.

One book on how to computerize a small business suggests that the owner sit down and figure out *all* the details of exactly what the system is to do. After all the requirements have been detailed, according to the book, "Requests for Proposals" (RFP) are to be sent out to various vendors. The RFP will be answered by a number of competitive bids, the business owner will select one, the system will be built as specified, and everyone will live happily ever after. There is no argument that this  "original creation" approach is the optimum theoretical avenue to a computerization project. The assumption, however, that mere mortals are going to come up with every detailed requirement and immortalize them to perfection before any system exists is not realistic.

The more honest approach is that a system evolves. Most users are not aware of this until they have been working with a system for a while. The first step of computerization is to get the main functions 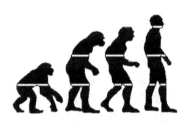 in a workable system. Hopefully this will also account for the major oddities and exceptional situations (such as shipping mythical widgets). After the system has been in use, the users will see that their jobs will be made easier if the system could just do "this little thing over there." The computer professional, whether consultant or analyst, programmer or independent contractor, modifies the "little thing over there" and the system is better than it was. Slowly the system evolves into an extremely useful and reliable workhorse. Trying to foal the mare and build the barn and plow the lower forty all in the same motion can be frustrating for the computer professional and heartbreaking for the users.

It is a misconception that computers will solve all the user's problems and that a system can be built in one stroke. But some misguided users want it *all* and right now!

Naturally, the professional wants to oblige the user. If the Computer Department, whether a team of experts or a single hired gun, falls into the trap of promising the sun, moon and stars deliverable tomorrow, that Computer Department has just slammed the door to its own cage. The user, in frantic haste, forgot to mention that sometimes suppliers bill late. The system delivered tomorrow will not meet expectations.

It has to evolve.

Another significant argument on the side of evolution is that users change their minds. To start, the user may say that a report needs to show who put money into the pension fund. After the system is in use, the user discovers that *who* contributed is not as important, for actuarial purposes, as the age and sex of the fund participant. Whether the system is a million dollar monster or a minor sub-system in a modest store-front, the fact is that the cost and effort of the "original creation" is never enough. Whether it is philosophically agreeable or not, computer systems evolve through constant creation.

When changes are needed, it is not necessarily an indictment of the computer professional. The change may be either a correction of an earlier mis-communication or it is a part of the evolution turning the system from useful to better. Evolution is to be expected and should be factored into the cost of computerization. Miscommunication is the cause of costly mistakes. A wider horizon is the path to a better future.

Another widely-held misconception about computerization is that it is an entirely technical subject. As has been seen, that is not the case. No matter how technically expert, a computer professional is a nerd if he or she cannot maintain adequate communication with the user. Computerization is an art as well as a technical subject. Maintaining adequate communication *is* the art.

Programming as an Art

"Art" does not mean a little frill that makes a system pretty. It does not mean fancy multi-color graphics. Expensive trifles may be enticing, and they can make a system better, but they will never make a bad system into a good one. The business person whose livelihood depends on computerization must come to understand the art of computing. Not that a business manager must master the art, but he must be aware that there *is* an art and be able to tell the difference between the artist and the nerd. A data processing department without an artist can, has, and will produce costly "systems" that are unusable.

The question "what is art" has hounded philosophers for centuries. Good music, an inspiring painting or a great novel all have one thing in common. Each produces an emotional impact. In the case of a computer system, good art will produce an emotional impact on the user. Every professional has stories of users bogged down in drudgery and the emotional release of having the software do it for them.

"I can do that?" the user asks.

"Yes," the software professional says and with the touch of a key, a tap on the screen, a swish of a mouse, the task is done.

"You have made my day!" says the user, and *that* is what a real professional lives for.

Technical expertise, of course, goes into painting a good painting or the design and development of a system. An artist must know his tools. If the colors get too mixed on the canvas, a painting will turn into a sea of brown. The artist must know the *techniques* to employ to ensure that his painting is not titled "Brown Mud Under Brown Sky." On the other hand, a mechanical production of perfect technical ability can leave the viewer cold – no emotional impact.

To another programmer I once suggested that computer programming was indeed an art form. With raised eyebrows, he declared to me that it was impossible.

"No, no!" he said, "It is a very technical subject." In further discussion, it became apparent that this "expert" had not, in fact, mastered the techniques of programming. Without a grasp of the technical aspects of the subject, the would-be "expert" was wrapped up in the details of computing and was nowhere near being an artist in the field. To become an artist, one must have the techniques of the subject come to him as second nature. That way, she can put her attention on the emotional impact to be created.

One does not have to be a great painter to appreciate good art. Not being able to read a sheet of music does not stop the shivers from going up my spine when I listen to Beethoven. Likewise, a computer user does not have to know the difference between a bit and a byte to get an emotional impact from a computer system.

The impact generated by a computer system is produced by the user's realization that the drudgery of his job is being handled by the system. As described under the Pareto Theory above, 80 per cent of any job is grubby, grinding toil that keeps the user from the creative and interesting part of the task. Release from the drudgery will would be a welcome impact to any user. The accountant in the firm should also realize that it is the 20 per cent lively and interesting work that actually makes the money for the company – the 80 per cent drudgery is just what "has to be done" to keep the business going.

For instance, it is necessary that a business send out invoices to customers. Looking it over, the invoice typist can see that it will take monumental effort to get the billings out. With gritted teeth, the task is begun. As the typewriter, under leaden fingers, taps out the first invoice, the user thinks, "Another night of tired cigarettes and black coffee; another night of no family and drooping eyelids; another night of miserable toil and desperate isolation."

Later, a computer is installed with dazzling technical perfection and hopes soar. Invoices will be able to be produced with a few taps on the typewriter-like keyboard. There will be no more sleepless nights! Oh, but the nerd who programmed the machine with such electronic certainty put the customer's address in the wrong place! Sure, the machine can impressively print reams of invoices faster than the user can spit, but not one of them is usable. The user puts in a frantic call to the nerd and gets an answering machine. The night-time typewriter is pressed into service again.

Though the program was a masterpiece of technical execution, a "perfect" program will not produce an impact until it makes the user become the master of the machine.

Technical perfection that bedazzles the user is worthless unless it can be used. That is why a user is called a "user." The artist who comes to be known as a nerd got that way by forgetting what the programmer gets paid to produce – something usable.

Later, the program is modified to produce perfect invoices with the address in the right place. A perfectionist computer whiz may grumble that the elegance of the program was ruined by the addition of that feature, and perhaps from a purist's point of view it was. But the user puts away the night-time typewriter, switches out the lights at a reasonable hour and heads out the door for the happy sounds of a warm hearth. The emotional impact, starting from the depths of a darkened desolation but ending on the threshold of a happy hearth, came about when the user discovered that the toil to be done would be handled by the system.

It is important to note that an impact is produced when that user realizes that the machine is going to do what the *user* wants. For instance, a user gets an idea:

"I wish to know who owes me money ..."

Rather than laboriously adding up columns of figures, the user punches a few buttons and *presto!* a list of who owes money is produced. "Ah-h!" is the exclamation, "My wish has come true!"

Quite an emotional impact – that is what the programmer is paid to produce – wishes that come true.

Where Dreams Come True

Since computer artists can make business dreams come true, the next step is to make them less expensive. It has been known for some time that about half the cost of a computer system is getting the software to do exactly what the user needs. That is part evolution and part mis-communication. Until the 1970s, most systems needed to be programmed individually. That is an enormously expensive undertaking, even for a smaller company with a modest system.

In the 1970s, some bright entrepreneurs got the idea that many businesses needed similar functions handled by their systems. For instance, many businesses keep Accounts Receivables (A/R). If a sufficiently flexible A/R system could be written, it could solve the business problems of many businesses, making many dreams come true at once. Also the cost of writing the programs could be spread across many users. Not only would the cost of the system be less to each user, but if enough users bought the system, the analysts, programmers, technical writers, and so on could make a lot more money than if the system were written one time for one user. The user's wishes could be satisfied at a minimal cost. Computer professionals could make more money. Everyone was happy.

But "canned" programs have never been known to satisfy users 100 per cent. Each user has a slightly different method of handling his A/R. A canned system could be counted on to solve perhaps 50 per cent, or even 60 per cent, of the individual user's problems. In rare cases, it has been found that a software package might solve 99 per cent of the user's needs, but there always is that one per cent that needs individual attention. The fact of evolution still exists. Hustlers of packaged software, at one time, tried to tell businesses that their Brand X Package could solve all the business problems the user had. It has never been so. Sometimes, with a package that is an extremely "good fit," that is, the canned product will solve 90 to 99 per cent of the business's special needs, it becomes absurd to try to add anything to the system. The return on the additional investment is too small to try to bring the software up to 100 per cent.

Pre-packaged software products in the mid-1980s flooded the market. If the user is a modest tax preparer operating out of a local store-front or a huge mail order distributor shipping from diverse locations on the globe, there are three, five, or 15 "canned" systems waiting to be bought. Some of the packages will be ill-fitted for the user, but at least one will suit the user. According to seasoned software buyers, responsible for acquiring software products for both large multi-national companies and smaller local concerns, if a 60 per cent fit can be found, the user has the best he or she can get. This means that some portion of the user's needs must be individually programmed. Even with the advent of smaller personal computers and versatile data-base and spreadsheet software, many business owners still prefer to hire "independent consultants" to create a system for their specific needs.

No matter how sophisticated future technology will become, I think it not too adventurous to say that there will always be work somewhere for a person who can make the user's dreams come true. Because of more sophisticated software tools and packages, the job to be done for any single user will be less than it was years ago, but because there are more users, the availability of work to be done will not dry up.

Since the independent professional will be expected to do less work for each individual user, the demand that the job be done right the first time will increase. The budget will not allow for costly mistakes. It will become increasingly important that the computer professional be a true artist. Technical skills will be required, but nerds need not apply. If the job is done right the first time, the artist is a hero; if it has to be re-done, the hero is a nerd.

The next chapters give the "how-tos" to be a hero, without having to expend heroic effort. The business person will learn what to look for to determine if that hopeful professional just hired is going to be a hero or a nerd.

Chapter 4: A SYSTEM IS BORN

Technical genius does not guarantee success for the programmer or analyst of smaller business systems. The successful consultant will be a computer ARTIST. As detailed in chapter 3, computer artistry does not mean "artsi-ness," but does mean producing an emotional impact on the user. The greatest emotional impact comes when a user realizes that the machine is going to do the drudgery that is usually associated with the user's job.

The actual work, the effort, involved in producing a system has been diagrammed and designed and graphed and explained in a number of good technical manuals on the market. These manuals give the computer professional a number of *technical* tools to make the computer more effective. What follows, and the next two chapters, contain the secret ingredients necessary to take the technical tools out of the realm of mechanical never-never land and put them solidly in the real world of the smaller business.

The major steps of delivering a system are:

- System Analysis,
- Design,
- Development,
- Testing and "debugging,"
- Documentation,
- Training, and
- Trouble-shooting.

Almost every system that ever existed skimped on Analysis. If 20 to 30 per cent of a project is spent in analysis, it is quite likely that the Design, Testing, etc. will simply fall into place. A composer once told me that in writing a symphony, if it is started correctly, the rest of it writes itself. That is ever so true in the art of creating a software system.

Analysis entails finding out everything the user (the consultant's client, the professional's employer) wants his system to do. That means every *THING* and *EVERY* thing.

The First Key to System Analysis

The analyst sits down with his client (the user) and asks, "What do you want this system to do?" or "What are you looking for?" Basically the question is: "what do you want to *have* from this machine?" The question is not "what do you think a computer is supposed to do" or "how do you think a computer works" or "what is a computer" or "how does your business work."

This is very important. The question that must be answered is: what does this client want to get out of the machine; what tangible *thing* does he want from it.

"I want to fly to the moon," he says.

"That's fine," answers the intelligent professional, "You will need a great deal more hardware than you have here, and you might want to talk to NASA about that. For right now, what do you want this machine to produce for you?"

"Oh, well, can it tell me who owes me money?"

"How about," the analyst suggests, "if it gave you a list of people who owe you?" The user nods that that would be fine. Notice that the analyst took a wish ("can it tell me?") and turned it into a tangible *thing* (a list of customers) that the machine could produce.

List of Accounts Receivable

Parenthetically, for the independent contractor, it should be noted that the example used, "people who owe me money," is the most common interest that a smaller business has in a new computer system. The machine, the software, and *you*, cost money. The system must pay for itself. Obviously, the machine must either make money itself, or it must help collect it. In a bookkeeping business, the machine will be used to help keep the books, i.e. *make* money. In a grocery store, it tracks inventory, and reduces the amount of money invested in keeping the grocer's shelves stocked, i.e. *free up* money. In most smaller businesses, a computer will most easily be used to generate billings and statements, i.e. *collect* money. At the outset, the analyst does not have to be concerned with whether of not the system will make or save or collect money for the user. The smart businessperson has already figured that out – or he wouldn't be talking to the analyst.

The first stage of the analyst's job is to discover what the user already knows.

Notes should be kept of *all* things the user wants from the system. Even if the analyst does not write down that his client "wants to go to the moon," he should be bright enough to tuck it away in the back of his mind. Perhaps next year, a new app will come out that computes moon orbit trajectories. Clients are always willing to hear from an old friend that something might be able to be done about that half-forgotten dream.

Every "want and need" expressed by the client is to be translated into a tangible thing the system can produce. Any indication the user gives of something that should come spilling out of his system is noted. Even if the client says it is not very important, is only dimly on the horizon, the desire is noted. Anything the client mentions more than twice, a good analyst notes *very* carefully, and is sure it is fully understood, because that thrice-mentioned detail is important, even if the user doesn't think so.

Suppose the client has mentioned for the third time that he'd "sort of like it" if the system could keep him abreast of the contents of the Floozle-bin on his shop floor.

"What about the Floozle-bin?" the analyst asks.

"We need to know how many ring-things there are in the Floozle-bin," the client states, "and what grade of ring-thing they are."

"I'm sorry," is the analyst's acceptable response, "I'm not familiar with how to determine the quality of ring-things, or the difference between what is inside or outside the bin."

"Ring-things," the client answers excitedly, "Ring-things come from the factory in grades A, B, C, or Q. When we get them, they all go in the Floozle-bin, and then we pull them out by grade to make Wam-jammers and Piner-benders. Wam-jammers use grade B and C, and the Piner-benders use A and Q. There are always some left over in the Floozle-bin, and we need to know how many of which grade, so we can order more of the right type."

```
Ringthings

A B C Q  → Floozle-bin → B C → Wam-jammer

                          A Q → Piner-bender

         (How many in Floozle-bin?)
```

The analyst may have never seen a Ring-thing and have no idea what a Wam-jammer is, but he can still make a note something like the above.

The astute analyst will ask the client, "Do you want a report of how many of each Grade of ring-thing in the Floozle-bin, or is it only necessary to know how many you have for Wam-jammers and how many for Piner-benders?" The analyst sketched out two possible reports.

FLOOZLE-BIN CONTENTS			FLOOZLE-BIN CONTENTS	
Ring-things			Ring-things for	
Grade A	50		Wam-jammers	45
Grade B	20		Piner-benders	85
Grade C	25			
Grade Q	35			

Drawn out for the user, she can see what the system can produce for her, and is given a choice in the design of the system. By seeing these "reports," she can see that she forgot to mention and also needs to know. The analyst can revise his sketch.

Frequently, the client will give the analyst a report prepared by the current system and ask that the system duplicate it. The analyst must understand the process necessary to come up with every number and word on the current report. Sometimes, the clever designer (see next chapter) will be able to short cut some of those processes.

By insisting that the client tell the analyst what the system will produce, it truly becomes the client's. By the end of the analysis, the vague hopes of the client have turned into definite *things* the system will produce.

The analyst should not expect to discover every detailed user requirement in one or two sittings. Usually, on a brief "trouble-shooting" assignment, the user already knows exactly what is wrong or what is needed, and a very brief analysis is all that is required. Most times, however, especially when the client and his analyst are just starting their relationship, the analysis needs to be lengthy. In analysis, the professional's primary concern is to turn the client's "I want" into *things* the system will produce. This is the point on which the analyst must be most clever. When the user describes a vague hope, the analyst needs to figure out the nature of the *thing* that will suffice.

There comes a point in every analysis when the client floods out a rush of things he wants from the system. Usually about the time the user realizes that the system is really going to happen and that the analyst is looking for (*things*), the client starts to envision more and more *things*. Rushing at the analyst almost faster than can be assimilated, all these things need to be noted down, even the most fanciful idea. The deluge will be paddled through later, during the Design stage.

While the cloudburst is occurring, and even before it starts, when the analyst has just the first hints of what the user wants, it is expected that the analyst will be starting on the design of the system. A purist would argue that Design should wait until all the data is in, wait until the analysis is done. In the best of all possible worlds, this would appear to be the case. A professional, however, will begin to get interested in the job, and will start thinking of ways to include each of the requests the user brings up.

The analyst is warned at this stage that if the "deluge" has not come yet, his design cannot be set in concrete. The design he is constructing is like ancient Egyptians – when the Nile floods, be ready to change everything!

It is frustrating to build a rugged but delicate design, only to have it destroyed by the client's new demands. At this stage, the analyst should realize that she *cannot* finalize the design yet.

After the flood, the analyst may sigh in relief and think that he can now get down to constructing a system that is technically aesthetic (what programmers and analysts mean when they say a system is "elegant" is that it is technically aesthetic). But not so fast – the analyst must still be ready to throw out portions of the design, no matter how heart-rending it may be to do so. There will be a few more trickles of requests. It is the analyst's job to pull these *things* out of the client.

The Final Key to System Analysis

Even when the user thinks there is nothing else he could possibly want, the analyst must continue asking for more until he gets the MAGIC answer.

"Anything else," the analyst asks, "You'd like from your system?"

"No," is the answer, "You have everything."

Notice that the answer is not "I've told you just about everything" or "that's about all" or "I don't think there's anything else." The magic answer the analyst is an unequivocal, absolutely certain "that's all!"

If the analyst hears "that's about it," he can work on the tentative design by putting together basic building blocks, but he needs to be aware that he does not yet have all the details. Coming back the next day, or a week later, the client may uncork a new cloudburst.

The pitfalls analysts tumble into can be very frustrating for all concerned: analyst, designer, programmer and client. Most all potholes and rough patches in the road to a good system can be traced back to two major faults.

The first is that the analyst didn't get the *things* the client wanted. The second is that he didn't get them *all* of them. The first key to system analysis is to get THINGS the user wants, the final key is to get ALL of them.

The experienced analyst will say nervously, "But they want the system to cook Sunday dinner and wash the dishes, too!" Don't worry about it, the job of the analyst is to make sure he got the things the client wants, and got *all* of them. Sunday dinner will be taken care of in the Design.

The secret of system analysis is to answer the question: "what do we want this system to produce?" That is true whether the system is computerized or manual, the command channels of a military organization or the work-space allocation of a love-bead factory.

Waterfall vs Agile

The above description of System Analysis was written in 1985. It has been suggested that it describes a "Waterfall" approach and that the "Agile" approach might be better.

Waterfall assumes that an entire system is being created. All analysis is done up front, then design, and so on down the line until the client signs off that the job is done. Like a Niagra of effort, the job is done in one torrent over the cliff.

Agile described a process of constant improvement, a series of smaller projects tweaking a system making it better and better. The client and contractor have to be nimble and *agile*, willing to switch direction when needed.

It is the age-old argument of Original Creation versus Evolution. (See the section "Original Creation versus Evolution" in chapter 3.) Is it better to get the scope of the entire project and make it all at once? Or is it better to answer the most important needs and then see what the next big needs are and fill those.

As with many things, the answer is: it depends.

It depends on what the client is looking for, the resources available and probably a dozen other factors.

Sometimes it is better to get the scope of the whole project and then take it up piecemeal. We might call that "The evolution of an original creation" or "Negotiating a waterfall with agility."

Even on a Waterfall project, after it is done, users will think of new things they couldn't see before. Clients and providers almost always use a little waterfall methodology with some agility. Any project I have ever seen that used entirely one methodology ran into trouble and had to temper the project with the other.

System Analysis above, Design and all the rest below will work in either case. The basic skills are the same.

Chapter 5: HOW TO DESIGN A SYSTEM

The designer is confident. All things the client (employer, user) wants the system to produce are on the designer's desk. The pieces can be fit together. Until this moment, the design of the system was tentative, hopeful, and, one might think, prematurely begun. But it is only at this moment that the design can be finalized. There should be a tentative design already sketched in.

Warning

Some readers may find this chapter too technical.

The next chapter should be more interesting.

Start with Known Things

The designer can take each item, each report, each *thing* the user requested, and determine if the sketchy design will accommodate the production of that item. Taking the example of the Floozle Bin Report, the designer might say:

"A program can be written to produce the report all right, but where is the data going to come from that tells us the contents of the bin?"

Looking at the tentative design, it can be seen that there is a file sketched in for Bin Transactions. "Ah-ha," the designer says, "The data will come from the Bin Transaction file."

From the different items (called "fields" or "elements") on the report itself, it can be seen what data is needed in the file. Because the report will deal with different "grades" of ring-things, then one field in the file must associate each transaction with a particular grade.

Similarly, the report deals in quantities of ring-things, therefore each transaction in the file needs a "quantity" field. From elsewhere in the notes, the designer discovers that the analyst found that the number received in a shipment is never more than 1,000 and that the number taken out of the bin is never less than 10.

From this, is becomes apparent that the analyst conceived the transaction file as dealing not only with vendor shipments into the bin, but also with removals of ring-things (used to make Wam-jammers and so on). There is a kernel of a definition for each transaction in the file:

Grade	can be A,B,C, or Q
Quantity	between 10 and 1,000
Trx Type	Shipment-in or Usage-out

A file built with this definition would record transactions something like this:

Grade	Quantity	Type
A	20	out
B	500	in
A	200	in
B	50	out

The report could look at each "record" in the file, count the vendor shipments as ring-things added to the bin, subtract out the ones used, and produce a report that looked like this:

```
FLOOZLE-BIN CONTENTS

Ring-things

      Grade A    180

      Grade B    450
```

This report matches the one the client approved previously, so the designer is satisfied that the transaction file has been accurately defined. Later the designer runs across the fact that pin-wamers are also tracked in the Floozle-bin and must adjust the record definition:

Grade	can be A,B,C, or Q
Quantity	between 10 and 1,000
Trx Type	Shipment-in or Usage-out
Item type	Ring-thing or Pin-wamer

Satisfied for the moment that the data definition is correct, the designer asks himself how the data will get recorded in the transaction file.

The simplest method of recording transactions, and the "backdoor" method for any data system, is direct data entry. The user signals the system "I want to record bin transactions." In its simplest form, an app asks:

```
       What Grade (A,B,C,Q) ?

                 How many ?

         Shipment or Usage ?

   Ring-thing or Pin-wamer ?
```

In the analysis of the floozle bin, however, the designer sees that the analyst has already discovered the only time that usages need to be recorded is when completed Wam-jammers (WJ) or Piner-benders (PB) come off the assembly line. WJs take two ring-things each and the PBs take a ring-thing and a pin-wamer.

"Since," says the designer, "we also need to record completed assemblies in the 'Completed Assembly Data,' we can also record that some ring-things and pin-wamers have been used at the same time that those completed assemblies are recorded."

Further, the designer sees that the Floozle-Bin Report is needed each time a batch of assemblies come off the line.

The designer discovers the only way to record completed assemblies is manual data entry. Same for vendor shipments. "Hmm," she thinks, "we could record these transactions automatically if we only had a Lens-o-matic installed at the entry and exit points. I'll have to mention that to the analyst. See if the client will spring for one."

Having traced the avenues followed by the items in the bin, the designer can map the entire Floozle-Bin System:

Data entry	Data Storage	Report
Vendor Shipment Assembly	Bin-Transaction Assembly	Floozle-Bin Contents

Starting from the report, the designer has traced every element that goes into the report, every avenue that item can get on the report, and by that, completed the design for the Floozle-Bin system.

The designer picks up the next report (maybe the 'Completed Assemblies Report') and pieces together the system that will produce that report. Along the way, the designer may find that the floozle-bin system needs a tweak, but those changes should be minor.

After all reports and "things" have been addressed, and systems designed and adjusted to accommodate all of them, it can be said that the system has been designed. But the designer's job is not yet complete.

Now that the design of the system is set, the designer can draw up program specifications to hand to a programmer. The programmer will uses these written specifications to "develop" the system. Because the designer has come to an understanding of how the data needs to flow through the system, the specific programs that need to be developed can be described with relative ease. For the floozle-bin system, the programs the designer specifies, and describes in adequate detail, are:

1. `Data Entry for Vendor Shipments: Ask the user (or Lens-o-matic!) the appropriate questions to record a shipment added to the Bin Transaction file.`

2. `Data Entry for Assemblies: Ask the user (or Lens-o-matic) the appropriate questions to record new assemblies being added to the Completed Assemblies file. For each recording in the assembly file also record usages in the Bin transaction file – WJs take two ring-things and PBs take a ring-thing and a pin-wamer each.`

3. `Floozle-bin Report: Go through the Bin Transaction file and add up the transactions according to the grade of ring-thing. Print the totals.`

Although understanding the flow of data is necessary to designing the system, of equal importance is defining the structure of the data, which was mentioned briefly above. This area is of such importance, it needs to be elaborated. How the data is structured will enable the data to flow smoothly through the system. However, if the designer maps out an unclever structure, the data will jolt and start through the system to an uncertain end.

Designing a Data Structure

Any data the system uses must get into and come out of the common "pool" or "base" of data the system maintains. This "data base" is managed by the system.

How the data will flow through the system in large measure determine how the "data base" will be organized – the "structure" of the data base. How the data is structured will determine how it is "managed."

There are a number of "data base management" systems and tools on the market. Even the simplest personal computer from the 1980s had a cassette player hook-up as a data base management system. Not real efficient – data was stored on the cassette and played back to the computer. Though not a very sophisticated, it is a method of storing and retrieving data from a "pool." Other computer tools are very elegant and are allowed the regal name of Data Base Management System.

No matter what the tools or systems being used, there are some principles of data base management which need to be observed. James Martin, from the IBM Systems Research Institute, has written an excellent book entitled *Principles of Data-Base Management* (Prentice-Hall, 1976). The book is a bit technical at times for most readers, but the section on data organization (Part II) is highly recommended.

Of particular importance is his assertion that, although there are many forms the data organization may take, the better ones will be able to be represented in two dimensions. The truth of this assertion is demonstrated in his book and is borne out in actual experience.

A two-dimensional representation of data will look something like a table. For instance, to represent the ages of the members of a family, the following "table" could be used:

Member	Age
Mr. Smith	42
Mrs. Smith	?
Uncle John	42
Jimmy Smith	17
Sally Smith	12

For each member of this family, the age has been recorded. Each record contains two "fields" or "elements." The first field has who the member is (Mr. Smith, Sally, etc.) and recorded along with that element, associated with that datum, is the second field, the person's age.

In each record, there is one datum that is unique to that record, there is one datum that makes it different than any other record. That datum is ideal as the "key" to finding the data. Because Mr. Smith and Uncle John are the same age, and it is possible that Sally Smith may have a 12-year-old twin sister Sue, the datum "age" cannot be used to distinguish one record from another. If we wanted to unlock the mysteries of the age of a member of the Smith family, the age would not be an appropriate "key." Each record, however, does contain one datum that is unique and can be used as a key to unlock all the data in a particular recording. In this case, it is the person's name.

Member	Age	Sex
Mr. Smith	42	M
Mrs. Smith	?	F
Uncle John	42	M
Jimmy Smith	17	M
Sally Smith	12	F

Suppose we want to add Gender to the data. Because gender can be associated with the family member's name *and no other factor*, this additional datum can be added to each record without disturbing the tabular form. The "key" of "name" can be used to "unlock" the person's sex as well as his age. The data organization expands.

This two-dimensioned table can be extended indefinitely by adding the family member's favorite color, whether or not the person prefers chicken soup to scrambled eggs, and so on.

Mr. Smith's family	
Relative	Relation
Mrs. Smith	wife
Jimmy	son
Mrs. Smith's family	
Mr. Smith	husband
Uncle John	brother

Let's add a new dimension to the data base by attempting to describe relationships between different unique recordings. For instance, to describe that Mr. Smith is Mrs. Smith's husband and Jimmy's father, and that Mrs. Smith is Mr. Smith's wife and Uncle John's sister, the two-dimensioned data base becomes hopelessly snarled in complexity.

This complexity could be pictured as stacks of cards on a table. One stack is labelled "Mr. Smith's family," another labelled "Mrs. Smith's family" and so on:

In order to record a relationship (put another card on the table), the correct stack of cards has to be found. Notice that within each stack of cards, the there is a two-dimensioned data base.

The trick the designer must master is to "smoosh" all these cards together into one stack. To do that, the "key" needs to be discovered. The question needs to be answered: what uniquely identifies each recording?

Each record contains a relationship (brother, sister, father, etc.) but these can be duplicated and will not uniquely identify a record. Each record contains the name of a family member, but Mrs. Smith's "wife" record could be incorrectly placed in Uncle John's stack, leading to incest. What does uniquely identify each record is the pairing up of two family members. Ah-ha, says the designer, the data can be organized around the key of "pair of members." The designer's data table will look something like:

---- Member-pair ----		Relation to Member
Member	Relative	
Mr. Smith	Mrs. Smith	wife
Mr. Smith	Jimmy	son
Mrs. Smith	Mr. Smith	husband
Mrs. Smith	Uncle John	brother

The data base can also be extended by adding more data which can be "keyed" to the member-pair, such as whether or not they are good bridge partners, if they could be a championship wrestling tag team, or if they have the same color eyes.

To organize data into two-dimensioned tables requires a clever designer. Intelligence is necessary. Although a lack of intelligence can be blamed for poor data organization, it is not a valid excuse.

It can be demonstrated that clever organization rests solely on the designer's ability to observe differences and similarities and identities between things. For instance, in looking at the jumble of data regarding Mr. and Mrs. Smith's household, the designer looks at Mr. Smith and sees a 42-year-old male and Sally Smith is observed to be a 12-year-old girl.

These two items in the pool of data are observed to be identical in that they both represent people. They have differing ages and genders, but they are similar in that they both do have *some* age and gender.

If the data can be looked at, and the designer can observe, simply observe, the similarities and identities and differences between the data, the organization will become almost automatic. The designer will also gain the reputation of a very clever and intelligent person.

Taking the Floozle-Bin example, the bin is seen to contain different items, ring-things and so on. Looking for identities, the designer finds that the ring-thing that entered the bin in a shipment is the same ring-thing that leaves the bin as a part of a larger assembly. Pin-wamers are similar to ring-things in that they also follow the same path through the bin. Wam-jammers and piner-benders (the larger assemblies), however, are entirely different in that they are never in the bin. Tracking the contents of the Floozle-bin becomes child's play once the differences, similarities and identities are perceived in the data. The design of the two dimensional "table" describing the data required to solve the floozle-bin problem is equally simple. The practiced hand finds that designing data structures becomes second nature.

Looking at the data being recorded in the bin transaction file, it becomes apparent that this data has no "key" because there is no unique way of identifying one record from the next. One shipment of 1000 grade A ring-things will look exactly the same as another. The two records will be identical. If it is necessary to "key" these records (a "key" is not *alway-* required for all sets of data), then some unique identifier will have to be included in the record. Adding an element for the time of the transaction might be sufficient in this case. The designer's data table would then look something like this:

FLOOZLE-BIN TRANSACTION

Grade	can be A,B,C, or Q
Quantity	between 10 and 1,000
Trx Type	Shipment-in or Usage-out
Item type	Ring-thing or Pin-wamer
Time-Stamp	When the trx occured

and the key would be Item type + Grade + Date plus, perhaps, Trx Type.

The Bin Transactions can be ordered (organized, sorted) according to any field. All the records of grade "A" can be placed together followed by the grade "B" records. It might be possible to sort the file according to "Trx Type," thus having all vendor shipments separated from the Usage records.

Organizing the data within a system entails the same actions as organizing data elements into files, folders, congregations, herds, pods or whatever you want to call them. The elements are scrutinized to determine their differences and similarities. But, as with the organization of data into files, some fields are more important than others.

The unorganized data of a system can be compared to a pile of beads in total disarray – the blue beads right next to the red ones. Additionally, some of the beads are tiny cubes whereas others are little spheres. Setting himself to the task of organizing these beads,

the designer starts sifting them into piles. But the immediate question is: Should the red beads be in a different pile than the blue ones, or should the cubes be separated from the spheres? Perhaps there should be four piles – one for blue spheres, another for red spheres, and so on. What about the other shapes and colors? As the beads are being organized, it is discovered that some of them are scratched. Should there be eight piles?

How the beads are organized will depend on the end product that is required from the bead-table system. What *thing* does the user want at the end? If the end product is red necklaces and blue ones, the obvious organization will be according to color. The element of shape (cube or sphere) becomes a less significant datum as the color becomes more important. Similarly, if necklace buyers want cubic necklaces, but care not about the mixture of colors, the color becomes insignificant.

The ability to determine differences and similarities is necessary to be able to organize, but the relative importance of each item must also be observed. In the designing of computer systems (or making necklaces, for that matter), the relative importances are determined by the product being sought. The purpose of organization is to produce a product (a necklace or a Floozle Bin Report). The product being created determines the basis of the organization. Do the red beads go in the same pile as the blue ones?

It depends on whether or not that would make it easier to make the necklace.

In the Floozle-Bin system, the designer sees that to produce his report, the records of the Bin Transaction file would be most easily handled if:

1) all the records of ring-things were separated from the other contents of the bin, and

2) the records for each grade of ring-thing were separated from the other grades.

Beyond that, to produce the report, the designer considers the organization of the Bin Transactions to be insignificant. Therefore, the designer will be sure the records in the file are sorted (accessible) by Item-type and Grade to produce the report.

In summation, the design of a data structure is accomplished by looking closely at the data that will be flowing through the system. Similarly, a close look at the *things* the system will produce reveals the data that will flow through the system, and how to "pile the beads."

How To Make Program Specifications

Once the data flow and structure have been settled, the designer will find that the writing of program specifications is a snap. The designer knows what each program must do to contribute to the overall flow. The actual written specifications can be very simple or quite elaborate depending on the level of understanding expected in the people who will be writing the programs. If the designer will also be the programmer (a frequent occurrence in a smaller enterprise), the specifications can be quite sketchy. If, however, the designer will be handing the specifications over to completely unknown programmers who perhaps have not even been hired yet, the specifications must be in sufficient detail that the recipient couldn't possibly misunderstand what is required of the program. But misunderstandings are bound to occur, so the designer should be available to straighten out any confusion.

In 1985, I wrote:

> I have found that the most easily understood program (and system) specs can be represented in what is called a Warnier-Orr diagram. Mr. Warnier and Mr. Orr developed this type of diagram from the "set theory" of mathematics. Any system process or data structure can be broken down into a set of sub-processes or sub-structures. These are graphically represented as sets and sub-sets.

That was followed with examples from the Smith family and our Floozle-bin. As I read that today, I did not remember using Warnier-Orr in the past 30-plus years. I had to look up and re-familiarize myself with the tools.

Factually, I have been using these tools and methods without even thinking about them. I can look at old designs I did for clients, I can look at program specs, I can look at my code from any project, and there it is – Warnier-Orr ways of thinking. I don't use the usual notation with curly-brackets and all, but the BIG IDEAs of hierarchy and sequence, repetition and alternation, and the rest is in them.

If a designer needs to write specs for a developer, and has no idea how or where to start, a quick look – or a deep dive! – into Warnier-Orr would be beneficial.

The level of detail required in these program specifications depends entirely upon the degree of understanding the programmer has for the system. If the programmer is an old hand and knows what is expected, too much detail will be an insult. On the other hand, if the diagrams are too simple, the programmer will not know what to do and may write programs entirely different from what was intended.

(The same can be said for writing proposals for clients. They have to be written with greater or lesser detail depending on the familiarity of the client with software projects and their interest in details.)

Warnier-Orr tools are particularly suited for including or excluding detail.

Sequence of Events

After the specifications have been put together, the designer's job is still not quite complete. Still needed is a plan of actions to get the system developed. This is usually a list of the sequence of events to occur in the development of the system.

Frequently, on smaller jobs, this step is overlooked because there are only two or three actions to be done. On larger jobs, however, listing the actions to be done is necessary. More than one software project has bogged down in backlogs and become so expensive that it was aborted before it could be completed. It would not be too adventurous to assert that the incomplete project was the victim of having omitted this step – list the sequence of actions necessary to complete the system development.

At the same time the required development actions are being sequenced, a time (or cost) estimate can be allocated to each action. Exactly how this is done is detailed in the next chapter, under "How to Make an Estimate."

It is important that the system be developed in stages. After the designer has determined the actions to be done to create a system, these pieces must be organized in such a way that they will produce a system that becomes more and more helpful to the user.

At the time a contract for a new system is drawn up, there will be a natural inclination to say "the computer guys will go off in a dark corner somewhere and produce this system to perfection and deliver it some months hence full-blown and without error." That is a mistake. As mentioned above, a computer system *evolves*. It is not a product of sudden Original Creation.

The first mistake is in assuming that the system analyst really understood all the nuances given to him in his interviews.

The second error is in assuming that the designer completely comprehended everything the analyst relayed. In the best of all possible worlds, this may frequently be the case, but never 100 per cent. In our less than perfect existence, it is an invitation to ill will and recriminations to allow a system to be created full-orbed somewhere across town or on another continent and hope it works to perfection the first time a user touches it.

The third mistake, even if the system is designed and implemented to perfection, is that the users can be *overwhelmed* by the sudden introduction of a massive new system. Confronted by the instant appearance of alien equipment and/or programs, the need to rapidly assimilate mountains of new procedures, more than one user has refused a new system – it is too discomforting. The would-be user finds that typing invoices all night is much preferable to having to wade through murky foreign waters, where electronic pythons lurk and the hidden quicksand of "errors" and "bugs" are rumored to abound.

Users prefer a gradual acquaintance with their new system. Users are smart. Once they get the hang of one simple function, they can be introduced to another one, and another. In this way the system becomes used – slowly at first, but as new functions are added, productivity revs up to a high pitched whine.

The final reason is based on good business sense. When a buyer, in any market, pays for goods or service, the goods and service have to be delivered – or else! Shopping for a living room set, a consumer will buy the furniture that will be delivered immediately. Rarely will people pay for the promise of hopeful delivery. Yet in software systems, all too often, users are asked to buy on a promise. Ever heard of *vapor-ware*? – software that never materialized.

If the furniture is not delivered on time, the user could cancel the contract. If, however, the set is to be delivered in stages, first the sofa, then the table, then the chairs, the consumer will be satisfied that progress is being made when the sofa arrives, and will be less likely to back out of the rest of the contract.

If software is delivered in stages that the user can immediately press into service, the desire for the rest of the system is sharpened.

Progress is being made. The contract was not a mistake. Both vendors and users can feel it. Emotional Impact.

The designer, in sequencing the actions for staged implementation, needs to first look at what parts of the system depend on others. It is frighteningly dull to order the programming of the Floozle-Bin Report prior to the existence of the Bin Transaction file. Before the user can see the report, he has to have data in the file. Rather than adding the time of programming the report along with the programming of the rest of the Bin System, and thus increasing the length of time that the user is going to wonder what is happening with his system, it would be simpler to program the data entry portions of the system, deliver them to the user and let data be entered into the system while the report program is being developed.

Also, the simpler programs should be given to the user first, for two reasons. First, they can be delivered more rapidly. Secondly, they will introduce the user to the system in a simpler, more gradual fashion.

The sequence of actions the designer would hand to develop the Floozle-Bin could look like this:

1. `Vendor Shipments Data Entry. Deliver to user and train them in its use. When the users have mastered this data entry function, they will be ready to dive into the more complex:`

2. `Completed Assemblies Data Entry. When the users have become comfortable with this more complicated procedure, they will be ready for:`

3. `Floozle-Bin Report.`

The sequencing of actions to be done should also take into account what the user thinks is the most important function the system will perform. If the user is looking for a Completed Assemblies Report and the Floozle Bin is only an after-thought, the sequence should be:

1. `Data entry for Completed Assemblies,`

2. `Completed Assemblies Report,`

3. `Data entry for Shipments, and`

4. `Floozle-Bin Report.`

The delivery of maximum impact in minimum time should be on the designer's mind when sequencing for staged use.

Chapter 6: HOW TO NOT LOSE YOUR SHIRT

Assume that a user/client/employer wants to have his system worked on, and that a computer professional wants to provide services. The simplest method for either party to lose one's shirt is to not have a contract at all.

The basis of any contract is an agreement between the two parties. The buyer says, "I want you to build me a house of such-and-such dimensions." The seller says, "I will do it for so-many dollars." The two agree that so-many dollars will be paid for a house of such-and-such dimensions. Without giving the legal definition of "contract," for all intents it could be said that a contract exists because there has been a "meeting of minds."

After the house is build, the buyer discovers that it has been painted a garish shade of canary yellow. He is offended and demands that seller re-paint. The seller balks.

As far as the seller is concerned, he delivered a house of such-and-such dimensions, *as he agreed to do*, and is owed his money. The buyer, however, never agreed to be stuck with a monster canary. It is apparent that an agreement never really did exist. There never really was a contract on the color of the house because there never was a "meeting of minds" on the subject.

How the courts would decide such a case is not in the scope of this book, for it does not purport to give legal advice.

But the fact remains that because there is no contract, either the buyer or the seller (or both) is about to lose big time. The fastest way to part with one's shirt is to have no contract at all.

For the computer professional, until there is a system design and it has been "spec'd out" (specifications have been drawn up and sequenced into the series of actions that will produce the system), there is no real basis for a contract.

The guts of the contract will be the design/spec/sequence. It is written as a proposal. It is a proposed contract. It describes what the buyer is getting. Add what the client is paying, and you have a deal.

The buyer and seller may have their lawyers tack on different terms to the contract, but the meat of the contract is still the proposal that the computer professional presents to the client/user.

It has been suggested by computer professionals who really should know better, that the proposal and all the work that goes into it is to be given to the client at no charge. From time to time, depending on how hungry the computer contractor is, this has a limited advisability. A "freebie" proposal will at least get the seller's foot in the door. Such a "freebie" should be recognized as an incomplete analysis and design (no one is going to do a professional job at speculative amateur rates) and will rarely make a good contract. A contract based on a "freebie" proposal may be legally binding but it will cause nothing but frazzled nerves and indigestion.

The Formula for a Winning Proposal

In writing a proposal, the first thing that the computer professional must, must, *must* ensure is that everything the user has mentioned in the analysis is mentioned in the proposal.

If the user only barely mentioned that he hopes this system will cook Sunday dinner and wash the dishes, it must be mentioned. It may be tucked under a heading "things this proposed system will not do," but the Sunday dinner will have to be mentioned somewhere.

Suppose the Sunday dinner was not mentioned in the proposal. After the system is done and the user is satisfied with what was delivered, the thought might suddenly occur, "We talked about Sunday dinner – where is it." The user might actually have had, during the entire time the system was under development, the mistaken impression that cooking was going to be a part of the system. For this reason alone it would be necessary to make mention of everything that came up in the analysis.

By including in the proposal every detail mentioned in the analysis, the computer professional is assuring the user that his, the user's, needs will be met. The user becomes more confident. Additionally, the professional, knowing that he has touched all the bases, becomes more certain that the job will be done fully and correctly.

Some might choose to term this a "psychological" advantage. Psychology has become known as a pseudo-science of mental manipulation designed to increase the domination of one person over another. Only the slow witted or criminal business person would stoop to such chicanery as a way of making a living.

Insisting that all items mentioned in the analysis find their way into the proposal is a sound business practice. It makes for a complete contract, leading to no fuzzy recriminations later. If the buyer, in the analysis, said, "I do not want a yellow house" that had better be in the proposed contract: "The house will be any color but yellow."

As previously mentioned, it would not be out of order to devote one section of the proposal to "things that will not be delivered." In practice, however, it is usually easier to include disclaimers within the discussion of what is deliverable. For instance:

> The house will have such-and-such dimensions. Although the buyer has requested that the color not be yellow, it cannot be guaranteed. Currently, the only color paint available is yellow. At the time of painting, the buyer will be apprised of the paint situation, and an agreement will be reached as to the color to be used or if no painting is to be done.

Or:

> The user has requested that the system cook Sunday dinner and wash the dishes as well. The remainder of this proposal deals with the cooking of dinners. With the current state of technology, cost prohibits implementation of a dish washing function. Therefore, it is suggested that the meal preparation system set forth below be implemented as is, and at some future time the dish washing function may be addressed as a separate topic. Dish washing is not included in this proposal.

Although both example disclaimers are adequate for a proposal, the second is superior as far as the seller and buyer are concerned.[*]

The first example merely covers the house builder's intentions, but leaves the matter open. At a future date, the buyer and seller are going to have to make a decision. If a future decision cannot be reached, both parties are liable to get bloody noses and part company whispering oaths against the other.

The second disclaimer, against dish washing, is absolute. Dish washing is not included in the proposal. But before the total denial was delivered, it was explained – the client is going to have to spend a

---

[*] Anyone can draw up a contract, but only lawyers can give legal advice. This book does not give legal advice.

lot of money if they want it. The client will appreciate the honesty and forthright protection of his resources. It may also just be possible that the client will consider dish washing so important that he will be willing to pay exorbitant sums to get it. The designer may have talked himself into a large and lucrative contract.

How to Make an Estimate

In order that a contract be profitable, the designer must make accurate estimates. There are basically three ways that a service contract can be worked. The estimate will need to be more or less exacting depending on the type of agreement being reached.

- The first type of contract is the "time and materials" variety. It says, essentially, "work will be done on the system, the buyer paying for materials used and contractor's time spent." The disadvantage of this arrangement is that it is open ended. On the other hand, the advantage is that if the user changes his or her mind, wants to make additions and modifications to the proposed system in midstream, he is entirely free to do so. The buyer thought a yellow house would be nice, then wants it green. He knows he'll have to pay for green paint and the extra 20 or 30 hours to re-paint. Because the contract was open from the start, the change causes no *kerfluffle*. With a "time and materials," open-ended agreement, estimates can be off the cuff. But it should be noted that estimates consistently short of the mark leave a bad taste in the client's mouth.

- The second type of arrangement is open-ended like "time and materials," but work on a series of properly estimated projects. The client can even issue a purchase order for each project based on the designer's estimate. This preserves the advantage of being able to change in mid-stream (with a change in the PO if necessary), but gives the client some control over the cost of the project. In this case, a too-small estimate becomes embarrassingly obvious when the designer must go to the client and ask for more money. A series of estimates that are way too large also can be an embarrassment and the client's confidence will falter. Most estimates should be fairly accurate but it is better to make them slightly high, charging the client less than expected. Be a hero. But when cast in the hero mold, it is a good idea to remind the client that the excess from this PO will be able to be applied to future minor modifications to the work just done and future trouble-shooting on the system. That takes the worship out of the situation, but still leaves everyone "with a warm glow."

- The third type of contract requires the most exacting estimate. It is the Fixed Bid. The advantage is that both the designer and the client know exactly what the system will cost and exactly what will be delivered. That is also the disadvantage. The user cannot make any changes to the system. If, in the Floozle-Bin example, the data entry program is delivered and in its employment the users discover that it would be easier to handle if "this or that" were changed, the designer is quite within his rights, especially if he is under a tight budget, to say, "It is not in the specifications." The program does exactly what the proposal said it would do and the designer does not have to lose his shirt chasing down every whim of the client. The scene can get ugly, but can usually be cooled out by the designer pointing out to the client that the program does do what is called for in the contract. And the happy ending is that the designer notes the requested modification on a "wish list" which will be the basis of a future proposal. It should be stressed that the designer is to fight tooth and nail any change to a fixed bid contract. If a change is necessary, it is because the analyst did not get everything the system needed to do (see "The Final Key to System Analysis" in chapter 4), or the designer ignored what the analyst had to say. An estimate for a fixed bid is reached in the same way as a "time and materials with a PO" estimate, with this provision: add 50 per cent "insurance." Thus, an estimate that might have been for $5,000 would be bumped to $7,500 on a fixed bid. Also, the client has no recourse if the job only cost the designer and his team $4,900 to complete. The extra money is to pay the insurance premium for the computer professional to take the risk that the project might cost $10,000.

If the designer has an understanding of the tools that will be used to put together the system, if he knows the computer equipment and is familiar with the language and the requirements of the system, making an accurate estimate will be relatively simple.

As the program specifications are being drawn up, the designer should estimate the time it will take to actually write each program as he writes the "specs" for that program. For example, in the simple data entry program to record shipments into the Floozle-Bin, the designer, who should be an expert programmer, might see that if he were to sit down and write that program, it would take him, say, 3 hours, to complete. But if it is to be written by someone else, even another *expert* programmer, the time is to be doubled – that is, 6 hours. The reason for doubling the estimate is that the other programmer must come to understand the specification and, in worst case, may write the entire program incorrectly and have to start over from scratch.

After a number of programs have been spec'd out and estimated, the designer will get to a point where there will be enough of a system to deliver to the user. Assuming the Floozle-Bin system is a part of a larger system, the designer may want to have all three programs delivered in one batch. His sequence of actions, he has determined, is:

1. Data Entry for Shipments

2. Data Entry for Comp. Assemblies

3. Floozle Bin Report

4. Deliver completed Floozle Bin system.

At this point the designer should have an estimate for each of the three programs to be delivered. But before delivery can occur, the system must go through serious testing and it must be documented and the users will need to be trained and there may even be some trouble-shooting required before the system can be considered delivered.

Take the total estimate for writing the programs and

- add 20 to 40 per cent for testing, depending on the complexity of the system.
- Add another 20 per cent or so for documentation – make it 40 per cent if someone other than the designer or programmer is going to do the documentation.
- Add 10 to 20 per cent for training depending on the designer's observation of the intelligence of the folks who will be using the system.
- Also, add 10 per cent as a trouble-shooting contingency.
- And finally, if the programming effort will be part of a larger team, add at least 10 to 20 percent for administration.

The designer's estimate will look like this:

```
Programs:
        Data Entry for Shipments          6
        Data Entry for Assemblies        15
        Floozle Bin Report                4
Total                                              25
Testing (30% of 25)                       7
Documentation (20%)                       5
Training (10%)                            2
Future trouble-shoot (10%)                2
Administration (15%)                      3
Total                                    19        44
```

Too many estimates would have stopped at the 25-hour mark, but the actual job will eat up closer to 44 hours. If, on top of that is added the 20 to 30 per cent that should have gone into the analysis and design say another 6 hours), the total will be hitting 50 hours. It is little wonder that computer projects are notorious for taking twice as long as estimated. It is not that the developers failed to do their jobs, it is that the original off-the-top-of-the-head calculation did not include all the incidentals – testing and documentation. This can be short-cut by simply taking the 25 hour estimate and doubling it.

```
Programs:
        Data Entry for Shipments          6
        Data Entry for. Assemblies       15
        Floozle Bin Report                4
Total                                              25
Double it                                50
Fixed bid "insurance"                    25
Total                                              75
```

And, if it is a fixed bid, add another 50 per cent insurance, which brings the total up to 75 hours. If you multiply that by your hourly rate, then you have your estimate.

At this point, computer salesmen and hungry contractors will be crying that they cannot come in with a bid twice or three times higher than a competitor.

Well, if someone is bidding that low, they either a) know how to deliver a better system less expensively, in which case it would be better for the client, or b) they don't. If the client can get a better system for less money, he'd be a fool not to take it. And the higher-priced salesman would be a fool to suggest otherwise.

But if the competition doesn't have a better mousetrap, they are going to be working harried sleepless nights for 40 cents an hour trying to get the job done. The way to take care of the competition in this case is to let them have the job. Do advise the client to ask why the competition's price is so low.

On the next job, your competition will either be out of business or be bidding at your price.

If the competition has been so short-sighted in their estimate, the job they do may also be equally hap-hazard. The wise salesman will leave the client with the thought that when the less-expensive job doesn't work out, he will be happy to return and pick up the pieces. A month or two later the wise contractor will call back and see how the job is going. If the job is going well, it might be a good idea to see what that better mousetrap is.

The end result of system design is a planned sequence of actions which, when done as laid out, will profitably produce a system the user is eager to press into service.

Chapter 7: SYSTEM DELIVERY

After the system has been designed, and the client/user has signified his desire for the system, as indicated by a signature on the proposal, the system needs to be

- developed,
- tested,
- documented,
- users trained in its employment, and
- deployed.

Only after the system is in the hands of the users, a well-oiled machine increasing productivity (and therefore morale) can the system be said to be delivered.

As indicated in the previous two chapters, the analysis and design stages of a computerization project are all too frequently skimped. The same can be said for the testing, documentation and training. The bulk of attention seems to go onto the development of software. The reason for this is relatively easy to understand. The development, or programming, of software is fun.

The programmer is a General maneuvering the resources of the computer, his army, in the battle against the forces of ignorance and chaos. He is filling in a cross-word; he is putting together a jigsaw puzzle. He sees the immediate results of his efforts. The machine responds exactly to his commands. There is no back-talk, no emotional outbursts. It is a well paid recreational pastime. It is very easy to be swallowed by the fascination of the total control the programmer exercises over what the machine does. The pull to fall headlong into nerd-dom is almost overwhelming. It is easy to understand a fixation of attention on the development, or programming, of the system.

Developing the System

Development is necessary in the delivery of the system. The professional, when starting the development of a new system, should first become familiar with the sequence of actions the designer has laid out for the completion of the system (see chapter 5).

"Oops!" says the programmer, "There is no Design Sequence."

That is the first thing the programmer should look for: is there a Design Sequence? If there isn't, the project has an infinitely higher chance of being killed before being completed. It is almost certain that a project without a planned sequence of actions to bring it to fruition will be more expensive than needed. Looking down the barrel of the gun labeled "no Design Sequence," the programmer concerned for his reputation and the future of the project should immediately take some corrective action. The exact nature of the corrective action will depend on the situation.

It could be anything from going on record – expressing concern to the person in charge – to taking matters into one's own hands, drawing up a Design Sequence and forcefully submitting it to the client in person. Usually, such drastic action is not required. On most projects there is some Design Sequence, however sketchy.

Having become familiar with the Design Sequence, the programmer (or lead programmer) entrusted with the development of the system should set to completing the actions in the sequence designated. Using the manuals of the machine and tools available, the programmer simply writes (codes) the routines and programs that will become the system.

When encoding the instructions for the computer to follow, the programmer is said to be "writing" or "coding" a program. The program specifications written by the designer should be followed exactly. If the programmer gets a "bright idea" how the system could be improved, rather than going off in some wild uncharted direction, the programmer should bring his idea up to the designer.

Almost any design, for instance, can be improved by making the system more flexible. Taking the Floozle-Bin example, the design may take for granted that only Ring-things and Pin-wamers will be in the bin. The client never mentioned anything else, but the programmer has an idea the bin may hold other things in the future. Rather than racing off, changing the design willy-nilly, the smart programmer will approach the designer.

"About the Floozle-Bin," says the programmer.

"Yes?" asks the designer.

"The system is designed to hold only ring-things and pin-wamers, but," the programmer begins to get excited, "One day, buggy whips may come back into fashion, and this factory will also have to store knuckle-guards, because those are used in the 'completed assembly' of a buggy whip."

"So," the designer cuts in, "Maybe they'll want to keep the knuckle-guards in the Floozle-Bin, right?"

"Yes," answers the programmer, "If the design, rather than specifying that only ring-things and pin-wamers are in the bin, said 'parts of assemblies,' then the system would be able to grow with future changes in the business."

The designer agrees, but adds the sobering thought that the entire design of the Floozle-Bin system would have to be modified. After rapidly sketching out the changes to the design, the Designer makes a ball park estimate of the cost to effect the enhanced design. In a pow-wow with the analyst, who talks to the client, it becomes apparent that this design change has come too late in the game. The budget won't stand it. The current design is good enough for the foreseeable future. But, the client admits, it is a good idea, and could be incorporated at some point in the future.

The developer is thanked for his intelligent suggestion and that it may be used to enhance the system later. The developer now writes the Floozle-Bin system according to the original design, but as she is coding, the programs are written in such a way that the future enhancement will be able to be easily added. Just because she is that clever.

Let us say it was decided to modify the design. Programming would go back and modify earlier programs – according to the modified design, and then continue using the enhanced design. Never never modify programs with some seat-of-the-pants design of the programmer's own invention.

Let me repeat that: Never never modify programs with some seat-of-the-pants design of the programmer's own invention.

The reason a programmer does not independently concoct his own design is that the specifications being worked from have already been approved by the client. Furthermore, the program(s) being worked on are part of a larger fabric. Individual initiative is commendable, even desirable, but when working with a group, everyone has to be on the same page. The outcome of the project is more important than a brilliant idea not communicated to all. Nerds may be brilliant, but the very defining characteristic is that they do not communicate with others well.

The program being written from the design may one day be modified. Future "bugs" may mysteriously appear, and the user may want the program to fulfill some function other than the ones known in the present. Because the programmer writing this particular system may have gone on to greener pastures when the future enhancements are to be added, another programmer is going to be going through the program now being written. For the sake of the sanity of that future programmer, as well as the future reputation of the current programmer, it is a good idea to write programs that can be easily understood.

There are programs and there are programs. Some are easy to read, others are a horror. A "structured program" is much easier to read than a "rat's nest." If it is at all possible, a program should be written as though it were following a Warnier-Orr diagram. It can be helpful to sketch such a diagram right in the first comments of a program, before starting to code. Sometimes a formal diagram is not required, and an old hand at the coding game can carry a diagram in his head. The fact remains, however, that a program cannot be structured (frequently called "top-down structured") unless it has been planned out before coding begins. Coding without a plan is a fool's game. It also makes dismal programs difficult to read and expensive to de-bug.

As each program is completed, or in the case of a complex program, each section of the program, it should be run through some relatively simple rudimentary tests, just to be sure that it does do what is expected.

"Truck Person" Guideline
(from Viken Nokhoudian)

A point I always drill into other programmers' heads: Our coding style is not to be the most clever and make use of the most obscure functions of the language. It is to be the most obvious, readable and most easily modified by other programmers who may not be familiar with the obscurities of the language. Your code must be for other programmers to read and easily understand.

I call this the "truck person" guideline. If you get hit by a truck today, another programmer can step in tomorrow, easily read your code and comments and pick up right where you left off.

To plan a section of code, write it out as a series of comments that spell out the logical sequence of actions to accomplish the goal. Then, under each of those comments, write the code that achieves that particular goal.

For instance if a program is supposed to take a series of numbers, sort them and then print the results, it would not be improper to write the routine that does the printing first. As a test, the programmer could feed her printing routine a series of numbers and see if they are printed correctly. After the print routine is working exactly as specified, the sort routine can be coded. Feeding the sort-print program a series of numbers, the programmer will be able to see the printed results. If the numbers printed are not as expected, the programmer can attack the *sort* routine, because the print routine is known to work. If each program, as it is coded, is run through this type of testing, and each does individually produce the predicted results, testing of the system will be much easier.

On the Design Sequence, there should be points where portions of the total system are to be turned over to the users. For instance, in the Floozle-Bin system, it was specified that the program to enable the user to do data entry of Shipments was to be done first, and put in the hands of the user. For the programmer, this means that that single program is to be written complete, tested, documented and in use before embarking on the other programs of the system.

When the programmer is comes to such a "turn over to user" point in the Design Sequence, and is satisfied with the rudimentary testing she has done on each program, it is time for "system testing."

How to Test and Debug

There is a widely-held misconception about software testing. The misconception is that for a test to be successful, it must uncover no errors. That is not the purpose of testing.

Testing is done to uncover errors, or as they are commonly known, "bugs." It is done is to catch these bugs before they start to "bug" the user. Pity the poor user with a poorly tested system. Sudden and inexplicable beeps, messages, and black freezes inundate a bewildered operator who thinks he or she has just destroyed an expensive machine. The purpose of testing is to protect the user from heart failure!

Another widely held misconception is that a system can be 100% bug-free. Testing can get the MAJOR bugs and a vast majority of the annoying little stops and "glitches." Testing can ensure that the system will operate perfectly under usual circumstances and even under most of the expected but unique and unusual situations. But, after years of use, after thousands of hours of operation, some user is going to come up with a totally unexpected predicament that will baffle the system – causing an error.

The purpose of testing is to uncover as many errors as possible. After testing for as many situations as a reasonably intelligent person can conjure up, and finding no errors, the system can be said to have been tested. The testing needs to be rough. The person testing must have in mind that his job is to break the system.

After running the system through a few "usual" operations to ensure that it will work under normal conditions, the tester must do everything in his or her power to baffle the system with bad data and incorrect procedures; see if she can beat the system, see if she can "slide one past" the system, see if the system can become so confused it just quits.

A useful book on the subject is *The Art of Software Testing* by Glenford J. Myers (John Wiley and Sons, New York, 1979). Mr. Myers gives not only the usual procedures of testing, but points out the weak points of certain approaches and suggests alternatives. His book covers not only testing, but also debugging – that is, once a "bug" is discovered, what to do to get rid of it. The book is suggested reading for the computer professional. Much of what follows on testing and debugging is covered in greater detail by Mr. Myers.

Testing and debugging are, or should be, two separate activities.

Ideally, the person who does the *testing* will be familiar with the design, know what the system is supposed to do, and have an evil joy in breaking things.

The best person to *debug* is the original developer. He or she is more familiar with the program and due to that familiarity, should be able to more rapidly and accurately fix the bugs found.

There are two liabilities to the original developer testing his own program. The first liability is that he has already programmed it to handle the situations he envisioned. Not being able to test for circumstances he does not envision, the testing will not uncover any "new" bugs. This is the type of testing that is expected in the development (or coding) phase of the system. The programmer is expected to produce a program that will do what *he* wrote it to do. Another person is needed to give the program unusual situations, situations the programmer never dreamed existed, to see if those can be handled as well.

The second liability of having the same person test and debug is slap-dash testing. Because the programmer wants to get home tonight before midnight, he may "test" with innocuous situations which produce no errors, and find – surprise, surprise! – nothing to debug. This is not a condemnation of programmers or an indictment of corruption, but it is an admission that people will, at times, be people. None of us is perfect.

A more fruitful method of testing is to have the programmer say, "The system is ready for testing." Then a person who knows what the system is supposed to do, perhaps the original designer, sets the system through *pre-arranged* paces. The tester, before actually sitting down to run a test, must know what the result of the test should be. Without that knowledge, there will be no way of knowing whether a bug has been uncovered or not. The tester should have developed before-hand a set of test data to feed the system, testing a maximum number of situations with a minimum of data.

For instance, in the Floozle-Bin system, the tester might have test data something like this →

This set of data tests:

a) the expected flow of data,
b) a larger shipment than the usual 1,000 items,
c) small shipments,
d) completed assemblies when there are no ring-things to make them, and
e) can the report handle a negative quantity.

```
Shipment
      Pin-wamers          1,500
      Ring-things (A)        10
Completed Assembly
      Piner-bender          100
Floozle-bin report showing
      Pin-wamers          1,400
      Ring-things          - 90
```

After entering the shipment and the completed assembly, the tester would print a Floozle-Bin report and see if it does show the expected quantities. This will test for the usual situation as well as for an unusual (but in business systems, not unexpected) situation. If the report does not appear as expected, she will note what the system did and what should have done. After finding a number of bugs (or running out of test data) the tester will give the results to the debugger.

Debugging

The debugger first tries to duplicate the results the tester found. If he or she cannot, the tester is consulted and the two work together until the results are duplicated.

Debugging involves two steps. The first step is to discover the source of the bug, and the second is to correct the error. If the Floozle Bin Report does not print "-90" it cannot be assumed that the source of that bug is known. The program may be falling down at any one of a number of places. By considering the symptoms of the bug, the debugger can usually figure out what the error is behind the bug. Once the error is known, the "fix" is usually obvious.

Discovering the source of the error usually consist of stepping through the program, following the code, seeing what is happening to the data. There will come a moment when the data is suddenly different than expected and that section of the program is inspected and narrowed until it gets down to a few lines of code. Narrowing is the hardest part – there will be times a debugger wants to pull his hair out because it just doesn't make *sense*!

Finally it is narrowed to a few lines of code. The debugger looks at what he wants the computer to do, inspects the code, and discovers where it is telling the computer something different. Once seen, the mistake in the code is usually obvious and a hand to forehead, head-slapping event. The debugger feels dumb for not seeing it before but fixes it, tests it on the tester's data. Hey! It works now!

After a brief happy dance, the debugger realizes his job is not done yet. The debugger has to go through a series of tests, as the original developer did, to ensure the "fix" didn't mess up something else. When satisfied it is good, the program is given back to the tester and the process repeats.

Most errors will be discovered to be fairly simple. For instance, where the Floozle Bin Report in the example above reported 90 ring-things but it was supposed to be *minus* 90, the debugger would probably realize that he had overlooked the fact that it might "go negative" and merely forgot to allow for that possibility. Going straight to the place in the code he needs, the correction is made rapidly. As Mr. Myers indicates, the error behind most bugs can be located by looking over the symptoms of the bug and then going straight to the needed fix.

After making his "fix," the programmer submits the program to the test data and sees that the result is correct – a negative 90 does print on the report. The thorough debugger will then re-test the program on other data to ensure his "fix" didn't disrupt some other function in the program.

If the error is not apparent from a consideration of the "symptoms", many errors can be located by "walking through" the code of the program. The debugger assumes the viewpoint of the data flowing through the program. He sees, first-hand, how the data is changed at the various stages of the program. Then suddenly, he sees where the logic of the program goes off the rails. Sometimes it is helpful to compare the program code to the Warnier-Orr chart that should be a part of the program specification. The chart defines the logic that the program is supposed to follow. The "fix" to an error in logic is also usually obvious.

If the error behind a bug is subtle and cleverly disguised, there are still a number of useful techniques available to the debugger. The final tool the thinking debugger will use, before resorting to brute force, is to devise and run test data through the program, testing for one condition and then another. If, for example, it is suspected that the "doodle-dips" (whatever those might be) are not adding up properly, the conscientious debugger will feed the program some doodle-dip data and look at the result. This will provide him with more "symptoms" that he can look at to see if he can discover the error behind the bug.

If, after having done all he can to meet the problem with reasoning and logic, the error is still hiding, it is time for brute force.

Brute force is a very last resort but sometimes unavoidable. Brute force includes the use of "automatic debugging tools" and the all-too-frequent recommendation: "put print statements everywhere in the program." Automatic debugging tools allow a program to be run, but to stop at specified "break-points" so the debugger can look at the data in the program. This is, in most cases, a lazy and time-consuming way of locating an error that should have been found by analyzing the symptoms. Scattering print statements through a program suffers the same deficiency.

Well, not quite.

There is one type of error which brute force will discover efficiently – the "language flaw." When a program is written in a higher-level language, such as COBOL, FORTRAN, BASIC, Pascal, C++, even LISP, it depends on the system software, the compiler and run-time system, to do the job the programmer is asking. Because testing can never be 100 per cent, even of system software, there are bound to be minor and very rare language flaws.

For instance, there once was a program which had the task of adding up a series of columns of numbers, get subtotals, then foot the subtotals and compare them to the total of the entire array. The program would take the same array of figures and sometimes say that they "footed" perfectly, and other times determine that they did not. The debugger was at his wits end. The bug would not submit to a rational analysis of its symptoms – because the symptoms were inconsistent!

Using brute force, the debugger discovered a "language flaw." Due to the difficulty in storing a decimal number in binary-floating-point format, the system software would sometimes add up 1+1 and get 2.0000000000012 or 1.9999999999998. This is a known problem with computers and the system software will usually handle this adequately. But on the particular system running this particular "footing" program, the answer to the question: "IS TOTAL EQUAL TO SUM-OF-SUBTOTALS" when both TOTAL and SUM-OF-SUBTOTALS equaled 2.000 would sometimes be "yes" and sometimes "no." The error behind this bug could only be discovered by brute force. No amount of logical thinking could divine the source of the bug. Once the error was found to be a "language flaw," the question was changed to: "IS TOTAL WITHIN A PENNY OF SUM-OF-SUBTOTALS" and the bug has never reappeared.

Brute force has its uses, but only one out of 10,000 bugs will be effectively handled by it. It is much more efficient and professional to mull over the symptoms of the bug and discover the error that way. Once the error is found, the "fix" will usually be obvious. If it isn't, the real error has probably not been found.

Sometimes a "bug" will be found that is not a bug. For instance, the tester says, "It didn't wash the dishes after dinner." But if the bug is not part of the design it is not a bug. The appropriate retort is, "Where is it in the specifications?" If it is not in the specifications, it is not part of the contract. Washing the dishes can be added as an enhancement to the system, if the client is willing to contract for that enhancement, but it is not a current bug.

The purpose of TESTING is to find bugs before the user does. The purpose of DEBUGGING is to find the error that is causing the bug and fix that error. The purpose of the whole testing-Debugging exercise is for the user – she will never know the bug ever existed.

Testing and Debugging is repeated until the tester is forced to admit that she has failed because she cannot find anymore bugs – the system produces exactly predicted results in every situation the tester can think up. The system has been tested on every point covered in the proposal (the design, the contract) and has been found to satisfy each point.

In chapter 5, it was estimated that testing and debugging should take 20 to 40 per cent on top of the original coding. Glenford Myers, in his book mentioned above, suggests that 50 per cent of the entire project can be used in this phase. To be sure, you may double your original coding to account for testing and debugging. A vague design or fuzzy program specifications, inexpert debugging or hap-hazard and inefficient testing, can make the process take much longer.

If the testing and debugging begins to take longer than originally anticipated, before shooting the debugger or tester, see if the program specifications are sufficiently clear for the tester to put together reasonable test data. If the system is supposed to report on the contents of the Floozle Bin, it would be silly to test if it can calculate the correct deductions from a payroll check as well.

The Necessary Documentation

The job, as they say, is not done until the paperwork is finished. That is because you are not building a system for your own pleasure. You are building it for someone else. Documentation is how you make it usable for others.

Without documents, the user cannot use the system. Future enhancements and trouble-shooting become impossible. The purpose of documentation is to make these functions – Using the system, Enhancing the system, and Trouble-shooting the system – simpler. Any document which does not contribute to one of these functions is worthless.

Without documentation, the user will not know what to do, the administrator will not know how to fix a problem and the client for some reason will not want to pay you.

Documentation is a necessary step many computer professionals overlook. The documentation effort can be – and *should* be – concurrent to the writing of the system. It can also be done in stages, along with the coding, or it can, though not advisable, wait until the system is completed. Documentation *is* a necessary part of any system.

Probably the most efficient time to document the system is as each stage of the system is done.

- As the developer finishes each program, the documentation for that program is written. The program is still fresh in the mind of the programmer. She can write notes on what it does and a technical writer can make those notes into usable documentation.
- When a series of programs are completed and ready for the user to employ (recall that the system was designed for staged implementation), the documents for that part of the system can be completed.
- When the entire system has been tested and debugged, the final documentation for the system is be written.

By documenting as the system is developed, the documentation effort is not a huge mountain to climb after the system is done. It is likely that the scarcity of documentation accompanying many systems is the result of designers and programmers failing to document the system as they went along. After all, nobody wants to go back and "finish" a system that is already "done." But, of course, a system cannot be considered "done" until it is documented.

The most important documents are

> User Manual
>
> System Overview
>
> Flow Chart

The most needed document is the "User Manual."

This manual shows the users how to use each program and in what order. As each program is completed, another page or two of this manual should be written.

Depending on how familiar the users are with computer systems, the user instructions can be more or less detailed. If users are going to be trained on the system (as they should be), instructions need not be more detailed than the example above.

The user instructions should include

- what the program is used for,
- how to start it,
- what to expect while running the program (including errors and handling them), and
- how to end it.

The next page has a user manual to enter Floozle-Bin Shipments. It shows the user the steps to needed to enter the data.

```
FLOOZLE BIN SHIPMENTS

To record shipments that go into the Floozle Bin, select
number 1 from the Floozle Bin Menu.

You will then see a screen:
┌─────────────────────────────────────────────────────────┐
│                                                           │
│   Item:       . . . . . . .     Grade:  . .               │
│                                                           │
│   Quantity:  . . . . .          Date:   . . . . . .       │
│                                                           │
│   Are you sure ?  .                                       │
└─────────────────────────────────────────────────────────┘
For "Item," enter the type of item (ring-thing, pin-wamer,
etc.).  The item must have been previously recorded in the
"item file" (see RECORDING ITEMS in this manual).  If it is
not, you will see the error message: "Item not on file" and
you should notify your supervisor.

If the item comes in grades (such as ring-things), enter
the grade.  Then enter the quantity of items received and
the date they were received.  You will then be asked if you
are sure of the data you just entered.  Look it over and if
it is correct, answer "Y".  If you see a mistake, enter "N"
and you will be allowed to change any field.

FINISHING: To end the session at any time, press ESC to
escape back to the Floozle Bin Menu.
```

The next most important document is the "System Overview." This will be used by trouble-shooters and future programmers and designers who will be enhancing the system.

The first item in a system overview should be a one- to two-page description of what the system does. This can be as short as one sentence for smaller systems. "The Floozle Bin system tracks and reports on the contents of the Floozle Bin." The next item in the system overview should be a listing of the project accounts or libraries in which the programs and data are located:

(FLOOZ1) – Programs for Floozle Bin system

(FLOOZDATA) – the data files.

Next should come a complete list of all programs, routines, methods, libraries and other software in the system, in some logical order and a brief description of each:

On (FLOOZ1):

FMENU - Menu for Floozle Bin system

FS001 - Data entry for shipments

FC001 - Floozle bin usages from Completed Assemblies data entry

FR001 - Print Floozle Bin Report

There also needs to be a listing on the data files used by the programs:

On (FLOOZDATA)

FBINT - Floozle Bin Transactions

On (ITEMDATA)

ITEMS - Parts and Items File

COMPASS - Completed Assemblies temporary file

These things are the bare minimum for a system overview. It is also a good idea to include any notes on peculiarities that a future programmer or designer should keep in mind.

A "grid" showing which programs use which data is frequently a God-send. Such a grid might look something like that below. When a modification is to be made to, say, the COMPASS file, it is easy to look through the grid and see *all* the routines that will be effected.

	(FLOOZDATA)	(ITEMDATA)	
	FBINT	ITEMS	COMPASS
FMENU			
FS001	X	X	
FC001	X	X	X
FR001	X	X	

The final can't live without it document would be a FLOW CHART. The flow chart, with its cute circles and boxes and diamonds, has been thought, for many years, to be a design tool. It is not.

Legion are the programmers and designers who surreptitiously design and write systems and then put together the flow chart and present it to the boss as the "design." Of course, flow chart aficionados find that charting a knotty problem in logic is helpful, and it is ... because it gets the problem on paper, it helps *document* the problem!

A better tool for design, in my opinion, is the Warnier-Orr diagram described in chapter 5. Flow charts are excellent documents for a system. They can be included as part of the "System Overview." To describe the minute logic within a program, the Warnier-Orr diagram is an equally valid document.

The difficulty with Warnier-Orr diagrams as documents is that they are not in wide usage. Flow charts are almost universal. With a flow chart, the flow of data through the system can be seen at a glance (if the chart is well made). On the other hand, if the data does not flow easily through the system, it becomes apparent when a chart is attempted. Crude charts *may* be made in the design phase of the system, and on knotty problems it is sometimes advisable, but the final polished chart is a document that finalizes the system, not a design tool.

Unless anyone misunderstands, flow charts *may* be used as design tools, but they *are* a part of system documentation. Please, programmers and designers, no more guilty consciences about charting the program only after it has been written and debugged.

The documents of the system should make it easier for the user to run the system and for future programmers to trouble-shoot or enhance the system. Only documents which do that are necessary.

How to Train Users

After the system has been documented, it is time to turn it over to the users. The users will have to be trained on how the system works.

The first thing to understand about training users is that they do not yet know the system – that is why they are being trained. This may seem just too obvious, but why else would a trainer get angry with a new trainee? Why else would the user seem too stupid for words? It is not  stupidity, it is ignorance. The trainer's task is to rid the user of that ignorance. Never never **never** get angry with a user being trained. To do so may prove to the user his own ignorance, but it also displays the trainer's incompetence.

The user must first have a purpose to being trained. The one-page overview description in the system documentation is usually the key to this. When the user reads this one-page narrative, he or she will usually light up and know what advantage will be gained by using the system.

The next thing to understand about training users is that it must be done on a gradient. Do not throw the entire system at a user and expect it to be immediately absorbed. Start with one simple function. After that one has been mastered, go on to another – preferably one that makes use of the function just grasped. If the user becomes giddy, an earlier function was not mastered and should be gone over until it is truly "under the belt" of the user. Sometimes a user might become giddy on the first step. That means that the trainer has started out too high on the gradient and must cut it back. In this case, a very simple talk of the "this-is-a-computer" variety would be indicated. ("The Four Parts of a Computer" in Chapter 2 has been useful to me from time to time.)

At all times possible, the user should be referred to the user's manual while training. For instance, when training on how to do data entry for shipments, the user should turn to the page in the manual and read it over before starting. When training on that function, the user would follow the manual. If the user becomes confused, the trainer should gently discover the problem and refer the user to the pertinent information in the manual. This is particularly important because the trainer does not want to have the users becoming dependent on him. If the user is constantly directed to the manual, he or she will soon become so familiar with it that the training will start to take care of itself, going directly from the system documentation to the user. The trainer becomes more of a supervisor of training.

The specific techniques of training above are covered in the *Basic Study Manual* (Applied Scholastics, Inc., Los Angeles, 1975) which elaborates on the points above and covers a number of other important materials of How-to-Train. The book is recommended for anyone who wishes to be a professional trainer. Any computer consultant should be.

Before the users start a training schedule, the supervisor should have a specific course of study he expects to follow. The training schedule will almost write itself if the system has been designed for staged implementation (see chapter 5).

When the training is done, the users should be so familiar with the system (or that part of it in its staged implementation) that getting a "final acceptance" for the system will come as a matter of course. The users know it works, and that it does what they expected, because they are using it.

After training is done, it can be expected that users will be asking: "Can we do this-and-that with the system?" These queries should not be shoved to one side. By thinking through the problem *with* the user (this is frequently referred to as "hand-holding"), the system can be made to cover new functions hitherto unexpected. From time to time, the hand-holding will not solve the problem, because the system simply cannot do the "this-and-that" the user wants. When that occurs, it is time for the system to be enhanced.

System Enhancement and Trouble-shooting

As the system becomes familiar to the user and it is not all-so-new anymore, a number of changes will be suggested by the user. These should be added to the "wish list" which was started at the first hint of dissatisfaction. It is not that the user is dissatisfied. Having mastered the current system, its future evolution can be seen.

Also, problems having nothing to do with future enhancements can be uncovered. The users should locate most problems with the system in their "parallels." Parallels are the maiden voyage of a system. During parallels, the users run the new system at the same time as the old system. The reports and conclusions of the new system should be the same as (or superior to) the reports produced by the old system. Depending on the complexity of the new system, parallels can run for a few days to a few months. During the parallels, the user will spot inconsistencies. These are reported as problems.

The computer professional must first understand the enhancement or problem the user sees. To do this, the techniques in chapter 4 are employed. The computer professional goes a thorough *analysis* of the request. He gets the *things* and *every*thing the user wants.

Sometimes it will be discovered that the system really does not satisfy parallel testing. It must be changed as soon as possible. A "trouble-shooting" expedition is arranged.

In trouble-shooting, recognize that some earlier step in the system development was overlooked. Either the analysis was scanty (frequently the case), the design was faulty (a strong possibility), or the testing was inadequate. In trouble-shooting, it is necessary to travel an abbreviated version of the original path of system development.

The adventure starts with an analysis as mentioned above, and proceeds to a modified design, a proposed change which is approved by the user, re-coding the improper portions of the offending programs, further testing and debugging, and documenting the change and re-training the users. It is as though a miniature system development effort must be expended – all the way from analysis to training.

If the modification the user wants is not to correct a problem in the original system, it is a system enhancement. Enhancing the system follows that same path as the trouble-shooting expedition. Even the most miniscule modification must go through all the steps from analysis, design and coding, to testing and debugging, documentation and training. If any step is skipped, the hoped-for enhancement will not be truly delivered.

There are a few details that should be observed when making changes to an existing system. The first is that changes *must* be made in some area segregated from the "live" data. The users rely on the live data. There must be "test data." Without that, the tester cannot manipulate the data to make fruitful tests. In the same vein, the program changes *must* be segregated from the currently working programs. For instance, a testing area might contain these files:

(FLOOZTEST)

FS001.ORIG - The original program

FS001.NEW - The new program

FBINT - Test data

ITEMS - Test data.

When the correction or enhancement has been completed, the changed program can go into production, but a copy of the original needs to be maintained for a while in case any unforeseen problems arise. The new production area will look something like this:

(FLOOZ1)

FMENU - Menu for Floozle Bin system

FS001 - The modified program for shipments

FS001.ORIG - The original.

If there are problems, the system operator need merely copy the ".ORIG" over the modified program, and the users are back in business – even though it is not the promised modified program. At least they are in business, even if limping. Then the adventure of "trouble-shooting" begins.

When making modifications, whether trouble shooting or enhancing the system, it is important to make only one change at a time. After one change has been settled, the next venture can begin. If more than one change is in progress, the two modifications can interfere with each other, making testing impossible and debugging a nightmare. The wise computer professional, finding himself in a battle zone of users contending for his attention and all demanding immediate changes, will make up a "wish list" indicating to each user that the specific problems will be handled. The pro will be taking them on one at a time. Get the *things* needed and *all* of them. Then choose one item and get that one done. If the user switches priorities in mid-stream, the professional will make sure everyone knows that the one that has been designated as a higher priority will be the one to be completed, but further priority changes could be disastrous.

In the face of too many modifications, the beleaguered professional might be prone to blurt out: "I only have two hands!" This is not the professional response. The appropriate message is: "All these jobs will be done and done properly. It would be a disservice to the user to rush through them or ball them up by trying to do too many at the same time. We are going for the best system we can get. It is my job to get that system. It will be done – one change at a time."

System delivery includes an evolutionary process of enhancements and trouble-shooting. However, there comes a time when the users are quite satisfied with the system and can think of no more changes. The original contract called for delivery of a specific system. That system was delivered when the users were trained and the parallels were satisfactory. But the conscientious computer professional does not consider that his job is done until the system has evolved into *exactly* what the user wants. The professional sees the user as the boss of the system.

If one cared to draw the distinction between the professional and the nerd, the line would cross this point – is the user the boss of the system? The professional would say yes. The nerd wouldn't understand the question.

Chapter 8: WHAT THE USER NEEDS TO KNOW

Most people believe, quite rightly, that it is the responsibility of the systems development team to deliver the system on-time and on-budget. The user, however, is also a member of the team.

A "user" could also be called the "client" paying for the system. It might be a business owner buying an e-commerce web application – the folks who will be pointing the mouse or touching the screen, *using* it, will be the folks buying her custom T-shirts. Or it may be a farmer regulating the irrigation of his crops and his field supervisor will be *using* the system. Or it may be a labor union tracking who was dispatched to which jobsite. Or it could be a bank whose tellers will be handling the accounts.

"User" is a loose term. It is anyone who will benefit from the software. The "client" buying software for himself or for the benefit of others, is arguably the most important member of the team.

You, the *user*, your first responsibility is to select people who are capable of getting the job done.

How to Avoid the Nerd

A nerd has been described as one who will "offload thinking and accountability" so she or he can "just focus on the work [he or she] likes to do."

The person is wrapped up in what interests him and doesn't pay much heed to others. When interviewing for someone to make software for you, look for these things:

1) Does he or she Communicate with you?
   Does the person ask intelligent questions? When answering a question, are the answers direct or does the person have to go

through a lot of back-and-forth and tell you the latest irrelevant theory from Professor Upchuck?

2) Is she or he willing to listen?
   Does the person make you feel you have been heard and then respond appropriately? If the answers do not make sense, thank the person and look for someone else.

3) Is he or she willing to learn new things?
   If the person is not willing to learn new things, you will have difficulty getting what *you* want across. This does not mean the person has to be willing to learn everything under the sun, moon and stars, because everyone does have limits. But the person does need to be willing to look at something new. Can the person have an interest in something completely different?

4) If you are hiring a programmer, if possible, look at a sample of his or her code. You want to be able to follow the logic.

Once you have a team, the user's main contribution to the delivery of the system is in determining the system's overall specifications and the overall budget. The user is also charged with the final acceptance of the system and its continuing evolution.

Viken Nokhoudian, a remarkable developer with a wide range of interests, wrote to me about what to look for when hiring a programmer. It matched my own 30-year experience. He has graciously allowed me to include his thoughts here.

> *When a developer is hired as an employee, it creates a long-term relationship that both parties must be willing to uphold. If the employer and developer each respect the role of the other, then great things can happen.*

> *A company should hire programmers that have innate personal qualities demonstrating intellectual curiosity, an agile mind, an ability to figure things out. When interviewing, look for the traits of someone comfortable in his or her own skin and confident of his or her own mind's ability to adapt to an ever-changing situation. That is the sign of a competent developer.*

> *A programmer's chief asset is not what he or she knows at the moment, it's the ability to gather information and implement it to do something new. That includes an ability to research, to communicate with users and a willingness to hear constructive criticism and improve based on it.*

When interviewing prospective programmers, I ask [the person], "What are the best qualities a programmer can have?" and give bonus points for a mention of any of the attributes above.

Hire developers who are knowledgeable about their craft. They don't need to know all the obtuse functions of a particular programming language - that's easy to look up. They should think in terms of user-friendly software, an intuitive user experience, reliability, efficient algorithms and user-proofing.

The developer should be able to think through how the software will be used and ensure the user can't break it by clicking the wrong thing at the wrong time, by entering invalid data, by doing anything that could cause a malfunction. Thorough testing of their own accord, then communication with test users, is a good sign. So, when interviewing, ask questions leading to their practices related to crafting software and getting feedback.

Developers have an obligation to write code that is as simple and readable to others as much as possible. After all, other programmers may have to work on it too. Beware the developer who likes to create obscure, overly terse, clever code that uses the little known functions of a language. That may be a 'hijacker,' someone writing code that only they can understand, blocking others from stepping in to work on it. That is an insecure developer or, worse, one trying to carve out a position from which he or she cannot easily be removed. Good coding practice includes readability for other developers.

A developer must be absolutely trustworthy. A lie is a warning, even about small things. Be willing to coach the developer, if there is any questionable behavior, but if there are more incidents the developer should probably be let go. Good character is absolutely essential, since the developer who lacks integrity can do significant harm.

Some employers feel affronted by a developer who is too bluntly honest, perhaps pointing out flaws in an overall software strategy or pointing out that the design team has come up with something that is impractical and will adversely affect the user experience. Be open to hearing this information. Experienced developers know something about user experience. For instance, the design team may not be as comfortable with mobile development standards as the developer [a real example from his career] and the developer can provide guidance. Make use of the developer's insights, if they are on point. The developer willing to speak up in an effort to improve the project is a real asset.

Not all programmers have a sociable personality. There are things the employer can teach them with a friendly, coaching attitude.

If the programmer lacks humility, suggest they be more considerate of others.

A developer who is easily offended by others or tries to dominate others can make an uncomfortable workplace and coaching would be appropriate.

If the developer feels insecure and tells a little white lie to save face, be friendly and let them know that's not necessary, that everyone errs on occasion and the goal of the team is to overcome that together.

If the developer suffers from burnout, ask what can be done to help the person find balance or stress relief. Don't force your own notions on them - if you enjoy playing Foosball, they may not. They may resent being handed a solution that doesn't work for them. Each person is an individual and finds stress relief in their own way.

Encourage good health among your developers. If they want an exercise space, that's a plus. It means they're burning off stress and can better focus on the job. If exercise space is not available at the office, the company might pay for membership at a local workout facility to be used after hours. The payoff is more focused, productive workers. Bill Gates of Microsoft understood this and his employees were gifted memberships at a nearby fitness club.

The best programmers want to perfect their software and know that the users are the best judge of its quality. As a programmer, when you hear someone tell you something could work better, thank them for it. Let them know such comments are welcome. Offer them one of your Snickers bars (you know you have a stash). That person is your best friend and will improve the quality of your product.

There is an odd trend among programmers to collect food at their workstations. Be okay with that. Software engineering is mentally stressful and burns up a lot of brain power. Snacks bring some emotional relief to the hard working brain and provide quick energy to keep it going. Snacks make the programmer happy to do the work. Bill Gates, understanding this, installed coolers filled with snacks free for the taking at the Microsoft offices. A programmer could wander away from his or her workstation, grab an orange juice or chocolate milk, and dawdle back to work or around the central garden pondering the next development task. It worked wonderfully.

Overuse of 'energy drinks' loaded with caffeine can adversely affect a programmer's health but be gentle, if you must mention this. Offering healthy snacks in the office break room is a good way to reduce unhealthy snacking.

Professional developers usually are not clock watchers. Your company may want to enforce the regular 8 to 5 schedule, with a scheduled break at a certain time period and for a specified amount of time. Normally, however, developers work in terms of project segments. They set a goal. They program until that goal is reached. Then, they may want to get up from the workstation and take a brain-break while pondering their next goal. They may want to work a couple of extra hours tonight with the understanding they may come in a little later tomorrow. If at all possible, allow flexibility for that work style.

The ideal employer/developer relationship will be one of mutual respect. Hire developers who strive to create the best product. Give them goals in the form of what you want the software to be able to do. Let them achieve those goals using their knowledge and talents to their fullest and you will end up with the best product.

What to Expect and What to Spend

The user should know what abilities will be gained by the system. After all, the system is for the benefit of the user. If the user cannot see any advantage to be gained by using the system, there is no reason to have one. This is common sense.

But the user cannot leave it all in the hands of the "experts." Computer professionals know how to design systems and put them together, but they are not experts in the user's business. The user must, through discussions with the computer guys, come to a

concrete understanding of *exactly* what the new system will do. It is the user's job to understand exactly what is being bought. The user does not need to understand what all the software will do, or how the hardware works, but must must *must* have a clear idea of how the system is going to change the work flow and whose job is going to be effected and to what extent. The user needs to be able to say, "Well, Josie-Ann won't have to add up columns of figures to see who owes us money. The computer will give her a list instead."

The business owner or manager, knowing what the system will deliver, should then be able to determine what that is worth. Without knowing what is being bought, there is no way to determine the value of the system *to the user*.

There are two fairly reliable methods of determining the value of a proposed system.

First, for a brand new system, where the proposed system will be the initial computerization, the formula is to take the annual salary of the people's jobs who will be assisted by the new system. In 1985, the annual salary for office workers was about 10,000. In 1985, if the system is going to assist the bookkeeper full-time (in other words 100 per cent of the bookkeeper's tasks will be assisted by the computer) but only half the secretary's tasks will be able to be assisted by the new computer, what should the computerization budget be? Since 1.5 jobs will be assisted (all of the bookkeeping and half the secretarial), multiply that by the annual salary (10,000) and the answer is $15,000. Most anyone in a position to buy a system should know the annual salaries of those being assisted. This gives a ball-park idea of how much to spend on computerization.

It should be noted that even *without* this formula, computer projects are deemed "cheap" or "expensive" based on it.

For instance, one man (in the mid-1980s) bought a used little machine for $2,000 for his office. His assistant used the machine for about half her tasks and the man himself used it for one-fourth of his jobs. The "budget" by the formula above should have been $7,500. Although the man was not aware of the formula, he *knew* he had gotten a very good deal and did not bat an eye to contract with a programmer to get specialized software for another $3,000 to make the system more useful. His investment was still only $5,000, and he knew he had gotten a very good deal.

On the other hand, one company (in the mid-1980s) had 23 people who were going to be assisted by a new system. The computerization project was budgeted for about $170,000, and everyone knew it was a good deal even though no one was aware that the formula would say that $230,000 was the "right" price. When the project was well along, the tab-to-date was added up, just because someone was curious. It totaled $190,000. Even though it was $20,000 over budget, no one was concerned. Somehow the system still seemed a "good deal." According to our formula, it still was. Later, when the budget got to $240,000 and $250,000, the screams started to be heard. The project was now "costing too much." Not because it was suddenly realized that the project was over-budget, or even that it was out of control, but because it had gone past the cost the unknown formula said was "right."

It is the user's responsibility to know how much should be paid for the system. By using the formula above, the figure might be $25,000 (two and a half jobs in 1985). If the designer comes up with a proposed system for $25,000, the user should reject it. Why? Because that is for the *initial* system and does not include any budget for the system to evolve. If the proposal is for $15,000 or even $20,000, that would be reasonable, but the business owner or manager should know that he really is going to spend $25,000.

After the system is in place, and modifications are starting to evolve, a different formula steps in to compute if the proposed enhancement is worth the cost. This formula is that the cost of the enhancement should be one-third to one-fifth the annual savings or income the change will generate. This can be looked at as a pay-back of one-third to one-fifth a year. Most people seem to find it easier to think of it as annual savings or income.

For instance, a new feature is to have the system add up a column of figures for Betty-Sue. Well it takes Betty now 2 days a month to add these up – one tenth her monthly salary is consumed in this column of figures. Betty may get $15,000 a year. That means $1,500 is spent to add up these figures each year. If the proposed enhancement will cost between $500 and $300, it should be done. If it is less than $300, no one should question it.

The two formulae above are used almost universally to determine if a computer project will be "cost-effective." Frequently, the formulae are not known, but they still seem to govern whether a computer project will be "cheap" or "too expensive."

Accepting Delivery

The user has the awesome responsibility of accepting delivery of the system. Some users become so frightened of this duty they never want to say the system is done. This is particularly true when the user is not aware that the original project will still have to evolve into the "perfect" system.

The duty of the user is to accept delivery of the system when it does what the design proposal said it would do. If there was no design proposal, if there was no contract then the user is in serious trouble. He is not in trouble because he "doesn't understand computers" or "computer projects are difficult." The trouble stems from a lack of fundamental business sense – no contract.

On the other hand, if there is a contract, the user is to accept delivery exactly when it has been demonstrated that the system does do those things set out in the contract. After the house is built is no time to start complaining about the yellow paint. Changing the external color of the system is part of the evolutionary process that the system must go through on its way to becoming the best system it can be.

There is one almost sure-fire test anyone can make as to whether the system performs as specified or not. This test can be done by almost anyone, whether familiar with the project or not. Simply walk around and see if the system is in use. If it is in use, it must come pretty close to the original proposed design. If it is not in use, there is something drastically wrong.

Some users look for "extras" in determining if the system should be accepted or not. Sometimes in the midst of developing the system, the user will mention something that is easy for the programmer and tester to incorporate. These extras were never part of the bargain. If the user got one or two, he or she should feel lucky. That another "extra" was not included is absolutely no reason to reject the system. Those extras that do get into the original proposal are there because the computer professional is generous and/or wants future business. Demanding too many extras, however, will make interest in future business plummet.

When the original system is seen to meet the design specifications – it does what the contract called for – it is only honest to accept delivery of the system. After the system has been accepted, the user will start to see its "shortcomings." What the user is actually seeing is the improvements that can be made. What the user is seeing is more of the "80% drudgery" of his job that it is time for the system to start doing. It was not seen before because it was hidden by the 80% that the system does now. The user's horizon has expanded.

Improving the System

Once the user knows that improvements are needed to the system, her next action is to find a reliable computer professional. If the folks who delivered the original system were reliable, the user already has fulfilled this step.

But if the original team was not satisfactory, the user needs to start looking around for one or more new software consultants. This can raise a sticky point of ethics. Occasionally, an "original team" will make it impossible for the user to hire any other consultants or programmers.

Please excuse a break in thought to introduce a few new concepts. When a programmer writes "code" (the programs) he writes in what is called "source code." This can be in COBOL, BASIC, C++ or any of a number of other coding languages. The source code is then "compiled" or "assembled" into what is called "object code" or "machine readable" programs. The compiling program translates the source code into something that machine can execute. When enhancements are made to the system, the "source code" is modified, re-compiled, tested, and if correct, becomes part of the enhanced system.

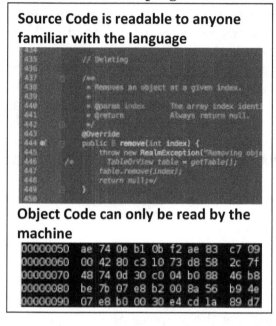

Source Code is readable to anyone familiar with the language

Object Code can only be read by the machine

It is possible for an "original team" to make it impossible for the user to hire any other programmers or designers.

This is often done by refusing to give the user the source code to his system. This is done by specifying in the contract that the user does not get the source code – or only gets the object code or only gets machine readable programs. If this is in the contract, the user should look over the people asking him to sign. When he signs the stipulation that he "does not get source code" he is saying that he is stuck with these software consultants and these ones only. If the system designer or testing personnel turn out to be unreliable nerds, the user is stuck with a sizable investment that will not be able to be untangled.

There are occasions when contracts of this nature are advisable. For instance, in buying super fast sorting programs, the programmer's fear of theft of source code and therefore piracy outweighs the user's concern over being able to modify or enhance the sort program. The sort program either works well or it doesn't. It should be tested before buying. If it works, buy it and don't worry about the source code.

On the other hand, a team of professionals designs and implements an entire system of 30 to 50 or 500 programs specifically to solve the user's computer needs. They can ask, and have every right to expect, that the user will not go out and market the system under the user's name. The user probably wouldn't want to do that anyway because it would merely be helping the competition. The fear of piracy is minimal. One obvious reason to keep the source code secret in a case like this is that the team of "professionals" have an uneasy feeling that they will be found to be unreliable and therefore must hold their clients captive.

Having found the programmer or team of computer professionals to use, the user should then sit down with them and relate all the enhancements he wants added to the system. These should be described as *things*. The analyst should note all these things down on a "wish list." After all the things have been related, they should be prioritized. The thing that the user thinks will help him most goes on the top of the list, then the next most important, down to the least important. It is quite possible that the first two or three items will loom so large that they will blot out the importance of all remaining items. The list of priorities might look like this:

1) Alphabetical List of Customers

2) Include Costs on Floozle Bin Report

3) all other modifications on "wish list."

As described under "System Enhancements" in chapter 6, the computer professional, whether a one man band or a team, will design the proposed modification, get the proposal approved, code it, test it, and so on, all the way through training the users, just as though an entirely new system were being delivered.

The entire delivery cycle, from analysis to parallels, needs to be done with the first item on the list before moving on to the second. The user should insist that only one modification be made at a time – even though the inclination may be to want it all right now. If the designers and programmers and debuggers all have their fingers in the soup, working on different enhancements, they can start getting in each other's way. If they do start tangling the job, other, more  reliable, professionals may have to be called in to straighten out the mess. If that occurs, the cost and time involved in getting the job done will inflate rapidly. It is in the user's interest to have only one modification going on at a time.

It is possible to effect more than one enhancement at a time, of course, but it requires a single design covering all the changes. It would be as though the wish list looked like this:

1) Alphabetical List of Customers and

Include Costs on Floozle Bin Report

2) all other modifications,

so that the programmers, documenters and so on, are working from a single design, from a single sequence of actions. If new personnel are put on the project, they will be able to pick up on the series of actions where it was left off.

The user has to know which things will make the system the most usable for the least cost. Knowing what to expect from the system, and what the system will cost are a large part of that responsibility. Being sure the original system, when delivered, meets the original specifications is also necessary. Seeing that the further evolution of the system advances in an orderly manner is part of the user's duty.

The computer professionals will take care of the gritty details of the development and testing and documenting. If they are true professionals, they will make the user's job of accepting the system and its orderly enhancement easy. But the employment of, and payment for, the system ultimately rests on the shoulders of the user. Therefore the user needs to take an interest in the things described above.

Chapter 9: STARTING YOUR OWN BUSINESS

Armed with sufficient technical expertise to make a computer stand up and sing, and ...

Using the ammunition provided by this book to create on-time on-budget systems that clients love to use ...

The independent software or hardware professional should be able to thrive in his own business.

There are a few rules of common business sense to be observed to ensure the business will flourish and you will prosper. These concepts are very few and, for the most part, common sense.

At first glance, some ideas will seem to run against the accepted norms that "everybody knows." For instance, it was once well-known that the world was flat – everybody knew it. Sometimes it is foolish to run against the knowledge of combined humanity. Sometimes, especially when the survival of your own business depends upon it, it is necessary. Rarely has it been found that the ill-conceived superstitions of yesterday can withstand the onslaught of the truth discovered today. Sometimes, different situations will insist that those agreements "everybody knows" be looked at in a new light. Besides, as my Pappy might have asked, "If everybody knows, then why ain't everybody rich?"

Other rules are not really rules but express my personal preferences in doing business. These concepts will be clearly labeled as opinion.

Those words were written in 1985. They are still true. Business, any business, has certain requirements that must be met. To do business

- Willing customers, or clients, must be found.
- Binding agreements must be made.
- Your service or product must be delivered.
- Payment must be made.

Everybody knows this, except the criminal. Some folks wonder seriously if national legislators know it. But it seems simple enough that everyone *should* be aware of it.

This chapter will deal with the business end of being a computer professional – finding customers, getting paid, and so on. Any rules, guides or suggestions I make are what I found that worked. You may already have methods and institutions that you use. If they work for you, keep doing them.

Getting a Foot in the Door

The first step to finding willing customers or clients is to let them know that you exist. The easiest and most rapid way of doing this, if you have any experience in the software field, is by contacting your friends, people with whom you have worked, and let them know you are available. Just let them know you are available.

"Hello, George," you might say, "I just finished the work I was on, and I'm available for another contract. I know you don't have anything now, but if you hear of anything, let them know I'm available."

For another example, if you just quit your job in the data processing department of the ABC Biscuit Company, tell your former work-mates that you intend to "go independent." The ABC Biscuit Company may become your first client. At the very least, if you *did* have any friends at work, you will get a few good leads to follow-up.

If, after exhausting all the leads your personal contacts made, also known in the world of sales, as your *warm market*, there is no work yet, it is time to promote to a *cold* market.

In 1985, a person could look through the "head-hunter" advertisements in the local newspaper. Newspapers have been largely replaced with online job-finding sites.

- Many use websites like UpWork. You can set up a profile, market yourself, and find your clients. Because clients also rate your work at the end of a project, it builds your reputation.
- Networking sites like LinkedIn are your online resume. Your professional connections verify your skills and give you testimonials. Do not under-estimate the value of a good success story. "Facts Tell but Storied Sell."

In 1985, I promoted myself as "No job too large or too small – I do it all!" At that time, anyone who could program a computer was a rare breed. However, because the market has matured, a person might market the rare skills. Your market is more slim, but they will seek you out, saying, "We've been looking for you!"

For instance, for myself, I could say I specialize in 3G languages on DEC or HP VAX or Alpha equipment. If you know that that is, you are probably looking for me. I also specialize in making sure your work force is nerd-free.

Using warm and cold markets, an experienced software professional should net a contract or two. Once a base of clients has been established, the software consultant can advertise for more clients, hire relatively inexperienced programmers, get larger contracts, incorporate and join the Chamber of Commerce. But don't worry about that yet.

The question, for the person who does *not* have experience is: how to get the experience? how to build up a list of contacts who can become leads to future independent work? This is usually answered by finding a firm in the field and going to work. It can also be answered, as in my case, by becoming a consultant at fees barely above minimum wage, with everyone knowing that you are new to the business and just building up. In either case, experience is gained by being in the field. One friend of mine started as a "go-fer" for more experienced consultants. In a few years, he went to a higher paying job in the data processing department of a local bank. In less than a year, he quit that job and from the few contacts he had made in his few short years, he found himself inundated with work. At the age of 23, operating out of his bedroom-study, he was billing his clients $2000 a week – a princely sum in 1984 and not bad for being independent for less than three months.

Everybody knows there are times when independent contractors go through "dry" spells. The dry spells only come from a lack of letting your friends know that you are available for work. There is no excuse, "everybody knows" notwithstanding, for a software professional to be out-of-work for very long. Some people blame "economics" and other external influences for lack of work. In days past, it was the alignment of the stars that influenced productivity. In the computer age, it would be hoped, such superstitions are behind us. "Dry spells" are not caused by external influences; the software professional just didn't let folks know she was available and then follow up on the leads.

Following up Leads

Alice, an old friend, just told you that she has heard that the Fairweather & Friendly is looking for people with your kind of talent. That is a lead. Call up Fairweather & Friendly. Find out if they really do have an interest in your abilities.

Send them a resume. My resume was never more than a brief description of my experience, abilities and a few references.

My opinion is that you do not need a thick resume. It should only bring up the points that put you in a favorable light. If you have only been working with computers for six months, don't mention your employment history at all. If you have been working with computers since the sixth grade and have been a software-related employee with three giant firms for the last five years, simply say "15 years in computers, five as a professional, see references attached."

The point is to keep it simple, direct, to the point, and honest. For instance, in my resume, no mention is made of my education, only that there are certain things I can make a computer do, that projects get done on-time and on-budget, and the reader can call my references if they want to verify what I say. I don't even call it a resume.

My opinion is that people want to hire me to do a job. They don't need to know that I got straight-As in High School. They need to know I can do the job. If they need to look at anything else, a "well written" resume for instance, then they want me for something other than the job at hand. I'm not interested. Not having a resume has never harmed my getting a contract. In fact looking over my 30 years in the industry, every job and contract was based on personal contact and showing I can do the job.

I've never starved for the lack of a resume. You have to let people know what you can do for them as a professional, but you don't have to bare your personal life or past irrelevant history to get a contract. If you do, you don't want the job.

Fairweather & Friendly may have a job they think you would be suited to. They invite you to an interview. Everybody knows you have to go to interviews to get contracts. I never have – I take that back – when I was starting out as an independent, I went to a few interviews with prospective clients. Not one of them turned into a contract. I swore off them. If invited to an interview, I politely decline, explaining that I am much too busy.

I will talk to the folks over the phone and if it looks good from there, then meet face-to-face. At the end of that, we both know if I am a fit and the only question is my pay rate. Or it is not a fit and we part on friendly terms.

Fairweather & Friendly has posted a job in my specialty. Ms. Smith is the contact. I call her.

"Hello, Ms. Smith, are you still looking for a freelance software engineer?" (She is.) "I believe that I could fill your needs but I'd like to find out if I really could be of service to you. What is the project you have in mind?"

After Ms. Smith gives me an idea of the project, I can tell her whether I would be able to work on it or not. If I can, we'll talk a bit about the importance of completing the project on time and other related matters. At the end of the brief phone conversation, I either have the contract, or I don't, but I make sure I have left Ms. Smith with a good impression of me for when she has other work – or knows someone who needs what I do.

It might be surprising the number of referrals that can come your way after declining a job because you really don't think you'd be able to do one particular job. People remember who has done them a service.

Whether the contract came from LinkedIn, an ad in the newspaper or from a lead provided by your network of colleagues and former clients, the time comes to take the job if you want it. The next question is whether or not you really want to take the contract.

Deciding to Take the Job

The only real factor in determining if the contract is desirable is in determining whether or not both parties are willing to commit the resources and energy to complete the project. In the case of the independent contractor, the software consultant, this translates into whether or not you have other commitments which will interfere with this job, whether or not you actually can do the job, and whether or not you want to see the client thrive.

Once you are satisfied that you have no other pressing engagements, you should look to see if you have the required skills to do the work. For instance, if the job deals with tele-communication hook-ups to distant sites and you are unfamiliar with this specialized activity, you could and *should* tell the client you don't have the expertise and gracefully bow out.

On the other hand, you can also learn the new skill. For instance, if the job is to be coded in C-sharp, you could say, ""I am not familiar with C-sharp but have broad experience with C-based programming languages. I think I could get up to speed on C-sharp in a couple of weeks. It's just another tool." You need to be able to learn new skills.

Finally, if you don't have the time or interest to learn tele-communications, but you do want the business, you can use your network of friends and acquaintances, locate someone with the appropriate skill, introduce the client and the tele-communications specialist and grow your business into another field.

Some people might worry that your tele-communications specialist could steal the whole job from the unwary contractor or that the client might try to cut you out of the job. This may happen from time to time, but believe me, any scoundrels who would stoop to such tactics deserve each other and the contractor who finds himself freed of such slimy associates should thank his lucky stars. It is much better to be bounced out of that contract before the work has begun than to be ten weeks down the road and discover that the criminal client has skipped town. Most people in the position of "squeezed-out contractor" would want to collect a fee from either the client or specialist – at least a finder's fee. That is reasonable, but if they maintain a cavalier attitude, appearing pleased with themselves for having shoved the original contractor in the mud, the contractor still has the most potent weapon to extract his reasonable fee – the truth.

Everyone in this business depends on his reputation. Calling a few of the people in your consulting network and simply stating exactly what happened and the resolve never to work with the client or specialist again will have a devastating effect on their futures. The contractor will probably get his fee – not because of any threats, not because of any blackmail, not because of any strong-arm, but because the truth can be a warning to others.

Before embarking on a reputation-destroying campaign, consider this: it usually isn't worth the effort. The contractor is generally better off finding another contract and getting back to honest work with honest people.

If, as is usually the case, Jones and the client are square-dealing business people, the contractor will be able to do the contract, farming out that part of it which is not within his area of expertise. Jones will be happy to be included in your network and you will be in his, and the client will appreciate the fact that you respected him enough to get Jones, an expert in that specialized area, to do an excellent job rather than try to bull your way through with poor workmanship in an area with which you are not familiar.

After ensuring that the resources can be mustered to actually do the job, the contractor must look at whether or not the client, in the contractor's mind, deserves to be helped.

 The contractor may have heard from his network connections that the client doesn't pay his bills or has had shady dealings. If these turn out to be true, the contractor is certainly within his rights to refuse the job.

The contractor may find, in looking over the client's system, that he has stolen, unlicensed, "pirate" software. I will never work with a "pirate." That is my personal position. Stolen software means that there is someone out there who has been victimized and doesn't even know it; someone is doing honest work, making a better world for himself and family and having it stolen from him without his even knowing it. I will have no part of it. Either the client gets the licensing straight, or I will not work. Period.

In two instances, I have discovered pirate software. In the first, I told the client what I had found. The client had been unaware of the situation, but tried to pass over it as unimportant. I insisted that as long as this piracy was not being handled, I could not work on their machine. The client got right on it, contacting the author of the software. The price of licensing was too high for what programs did. The client had me erase it from their system. When it was erased, the "piracy" was ended.

In the second case of piracy, the client had bought software to run on one computer. In time, it was transferred to run also on another computer. This was not within the bounds on the license, which was for "one computer." It was planned to buy a bigger computer, and put both systems back on one machine. I called the software owners who had issued the license and informed them of the situation. Their legal department (part of my personal network) said that under the circumstances, they would let it pass. If the people who own the software aren't worried about the minor infraction of the license, I won't either.

I won't knowingly work for a pirate. If for no other reason, someone with a pirate mentality is liable to slit my throat when I'm not looking. Working for a pirate, I'd say, is asking for trouble.

You, as a contractor, have personal preferences as well. Some clients do not deserve your attention. Some people would refuse to work for a pornographer. Others would not want to work for the Army or Air Force, but wouldn't mind taking a contract with the Coast Guard. Although part of being a professional is to not let personal feelings interfere with professional judgments, there are times to refuse a job rather than do something immoral. For example, if the contractor feels that pornography is wrong, it would not stop him or her from doing a good, professional, workman-like job on a mailing list for a company specializing in "plain brown wrappers." The contract is simple enough. The contract could be done. But would the contractor still respect himself (or herself) the next morning? If the answer is "no," don't take the job.

Assuming that the contractor has determined that she is able to take the job, that is,

1) no other pressing engagements,
2) has the required technical expertise, and
3) is willing to see the client thrive,

it is necessary to determine if the client is ready to commit the required resources. This is easily done.

The contractor, having heard the basic requirements of the system, makes a mental design encompassing the major points. This is done very rapidly – even in the first meeting with the client. The contractor makes a "ball-park" estimate of the cost involved to the client, including the design and programming and testing and documentation and parallel runs. This figure is upped by at least 50 per cent (because not all the analysis or design has been done and it is better to be on the high side) and given to the client as a rough – very rough – estimate.

The client will either gasp and grab his chest in feigned heart failure, or he will calmly consent that it would be well worth it. In the case of calm consent, the contractor is ready to do a full analysis and design and come back with a more exact cost. In the case of heart failure, the project can be broken down and fed piecemeal to the client:

"The cost for the entire package would be $165,000." (another gasp, not quite as loud) "But that is for the entire package. Perhaps we are not ready for that big a bite. You said you wanted three things here – improved customer billing, floozle bin reporting, and full-scale employee security with software and hardware. We could go this one step at a time.

"Improved customer billing on the scale you mentioned is roughly estimated at $5,000. Floozle bin reporting is about $10,000. The employee security system is about $150,000. Perhaps we could forego the employee security and just do the billing enhancements and bin reporting for the $15,000."

The client will sigh in relief and may well give the go-ahead to design the first two. He may try to talk you down to $10,000 for both the customer billing and floozle bin reporting. You can say you'll see what you can do, but never back down from an estimate once given.

Never Back Down from an Estimate

The only reason to back down from an honest estimate is because you think you need this client. You don't. If you have made an honest estimate, the invitation to lower the estimate is an invitation to cut your own throat. If you succumb to the urge "to please the client" it is because you don't believe your own ability to estimate or the value of your abilities.

Clients sense this. If you back down from an estimate, the client knows either (a) you don't know what you are doing, (b) you don't think you know what you are doing, or (c) both. He wants to hire someone who can get the job done. When you lower the estimate, he knows that you'll either starve getting the job done or you are too ignorant to get it done. NEVER NEVER NEVER back down from an estimate once given.

On the other side of that coin is the rule to never cut an honest estimate just to get the job. If you do, it means *you* think your services are over-priced and you better let some air out of your over-inflated self-importance.

If, after presenting the client with the "ball-park" estimate, he does not want to go ahead with the project, you are both better off ending the discussion right there. He doesn't need you if it is going to cost too much. You don't need him if he can't appreciate what you are giving him.

It has been suggested that the way to present estimates is to do it a little piece at a time. This would mean to estimate a small amount, even a "loss leader" (less than you would normally charge) to do an analysis and design and then the bulk of the estimate only after the design is done. This has the advantage, some say, of allowing the client to bite off small enough amounts and get into the swing of the project and get gradually committed to it thus making it not "too hard" on the client – like getting into cold water one toe at a time.

This sounds to me like a manipulative psychological ploy made to sound reasonable by the "one toe in the water" analogy. It starts with the assumption that the client is some kind of pansy who can't stand the shock of hard business decisions. Next is the idea that if the client is not a pansy, your services aren't worth the money because an honest estimate will be rejected. The final absurdity of this approach is that the "loss leader" design will probably be slip-shod because professionals do not do their best work at amateur rates. Therefore the final estimate based on the "design" will probably be wrong. After that money runs out, the computer team will have to come back asking for more money. It is no wonder to me that clients manipulated with this kind of psychological clap-trap will not want to have anything to do with the "flakes" who call themselves computer professionals.

Much better is the honest approach: "I think it will cost $165,000" (Gasp) "It could be less, but that is in the ball-park. A full design will probably cost about $10,000 and I could then give you an exact figure."

The client answers, "I can't spend any more than $90,000 for the whole project."

"That will be kept in mind," the honest computer professional says. "I will do the design and estimate. It will be designed for staged implementation. Some functions will certainly be optional – you may even see some functions you thought you wanted, but discover they are unimportant. All functions will be included in the design, including their costs. If you decide to forego one or more options, the price will be reduced appropriately. I think we can get you most of what you want, possibly *all* the important functions, within your budget."

"Alright," the client says, "I'll buy the design." Or, "No, I think I'll shop around."

In either case, your response is, "No problem."

If the client is shopping around, call back in a month or so, unless you have become too busy and just can't follow up on it, and ask how the shopping is going.

There may be someone who is doing it at half the cost. "Wow!" you think, and see if you can arrange to see how they are doing it. Maybe you could learn something. Or the client may ask if you could do the design after all because you were the only one who seemed to know what you were doing. What that translates to is that you were the only one who treated the client with respect and not like some psychological test-mouse to be manipulated through a maze.

Getting Down to Business

Having decided to take the job because you can devote the time and skills required, and the client is committed to spend the money and time, the next point is to fulfill the design contract. Get that design done exactly as the two of you agreed – exactly on time and on budget – as if your life depended on it. It does. Exert every effort to fulfill your obligations to the contract. Attend to every detail. Work through sleepless nights if necessary. Forget your spouse and children if you have to. Do a job that you know no one could do better. At the end will be a design of which you can be proud. And an estimate you know will be able to be met on time and on budget.

But what if, doing all you can, you see that this five-week design contract is going to take a little longer. As soon as you are aware of it, go to the client and tell him or her – immediately.

"I know the design is supposed to be done April tenth," you say, "For $10,000. Because of the added floozle bin requirements we didn't know about when this started, it is going to take a few days longer – probably to April 15th – and cost about $12,000."

"Oh." The client is not real happy. He wants to present the design to the Board of Directors on the 20th and five days is not going to be enough time to digest the design and estimate. The extra two grand will not make them very happy either.

"I'm not happy about this either," you say. "The unknown requirements have added quite a bit to the effort. I want to get you an excellent product for your Board of Directors meeting on the 20th. Set aside some time on the 15th, and I will not only give you the report, but we'll go over it together."

The client puckers his lips. "OK, but I told them the design would be $10,000. If you can take that other $2,000 and put it – like 'To complete design $2,000' – it will go over OK."

It is the designer's turn to purse lips. "I don't like it – can we say that even if the rest of the design is rejected, the $2,000 will be paid?"

"No promises, sorry."

"Well," says the business-wise designer, "This design is valuable to your firm. Even if you don't hire me and my company to complete the project, the design would be useful to you. You could hire high-school students at half the rate to get some experience and set them to this design and they could do it at, perhaps, less cost." The client nods. "So," you say, "I am going to retain ownership and copyright to the design until the full amount is paid. When it is paid, you buy full rights to it and *can* hire anyone you want to complete the project."

"That's not a bad idea," says the client as if seeing a new idea on the horizon. "Would you, personally, train and oversee some students we hire?"

The designer, mentally surveying his commitments, and seeing that the proposal does not conflict with any, answers, "Sure. It's not how I intended to get the job done. It may cost you less, but would almost certainly take more time because we'd have inexperienced programmers. Would that be alright?"

"I'll think it over. Right now just finish the design, and we'll go over it on the 15th."

On the 15th, the designer hands the completed design to the client, with a big "copyright" notice on the title page. They go over it. At the end of the design and estimate is a paragraph:

"This estimate is based on experienced computer professionals doing the work. It is possible that inexperienced students could be recruited to do the job. If that route is taken, the monetary cost of implementing the system could be less. The time elapsed to complete the job, however, is likely to increase."

The design and estimate rarely give opinions as to the best route to take. The client is to be trusted to make the correct decisions for his business. The computer professional's job is to present the facts.

The client will comb through the design. Some options will be taken, others rejected. In all likelihood, most of the design will be accepted as is. There may be a few modifications. The proposal (design and estimate) become the basis for the contract to complete the project.

After the proposal is accepted, it it your job to fulfill the contract. You wrote it, you can do it – exactly on time and on budget – your life depends on it. Exert every effort. Attend to every detail. Sleepless nights should not be necessary, but if they are, sleep after the job is done. At the end will be a system of which you can be proud.

Getting Paid

While the job is being done, either the design or the development of the actual system, make sure you are being paid. Different clients have different requirements. For most, you should be able to submit a monthly invoice, or perhaps weekly, and be paid within a week or so. Work out the exact mechanics of payment beforehand.

If you are to submit a weekly invoice which will be paid in 30 days, and you can live with that arrangement, submit your invoices and continue working for 30 days.

If payment is late, bring it up to the client. If it continues being late, stop working. You have better things to do than work for free. You are a professional. That means you get paid for your services. If you don't, you don't want to be where you are not appreciated.

Sometimes, you have to get tough. If the agreement is that you are to be paid every Monday for the invoice you turned in last Friday, and Monday came and went without a check, on Tuesday morning show up at the accountant's desk asking where your check is. If it is not forthcoming, go to the boss and tell him that neither he nor you has the time to waste on this sort of foolishness. If the check is still not forthcoming, tell the client you have better things to do, and when the check is ready to give you a call – you'll be working for someone else. If the check is still not forthcoming, you're better off without that "client." Later on, you may get a call from Joe, one of your network associates asking about the design.

"Say, about that floozle bin design you did for Blodgett & Company, I have a question," says Joe.

"Joe, you're working for Fred Blodgett now?"

"Yes, on the floozle bins – " Joe changes ideas, "Say, you know they weren't too happy about your sudden leaving. Said some pretty nasty things about you. What happened?"

"They owe me and won't pay," you answer. "Have they paid you yet?"

"No, they're supposed to next Tuesday." Joe thinks about the fact that you haven't been paid yet and wonders what might happen next Tuesday.

It doesn't take much to get paid, if you do honest work. Most people are as honest as you are. If the client won't pay for your honest labor, well, it's like the Good Book says: criminal loot slits the throat of he who is greedy for it (loose translation of Proverbs 1:19). Being as honest as you can gives you the perception to see when someone else is not honest. They say you can't cheat an honest man. The criminals dig their own graves. You don't have to grab a shovel and dig your own ditch. You'll only be cheating yourself.

The Secret Skills

To succeed as a computer professional, you will need technical expertise. It will be necessary to know how a computer works and what can be done to manipulate the various pieces of hardware and software. When working on a specific system, you will have to be familiar with the technical manuals of that system. Using the information in those manuals will enable you to push the system to its limits in obtaining a useful tool for your client. As mentioned in chapter 1, libraries have been written on the techniques of programming and the tricks of manipulating bits and bytes, disk drives and memory. It is necessary for the computer professional to have a firm grounding in the fundamental technical aspects of computers.

To gain the firm grounding and to build a storehouse of expertise on that ground, the computer professional needs the ability to study. This is a subject largely ignored by modern education – just how does one study? In chapter 7, under the heading "How to Train Users," is mentioned a book, the *Basic Study Manual*, which covers the "how-tos" of study itself. The user needs to be able to learn how to use the system. The computer professional needs to be able to learn about computers and keep up with a rapidly changing subject.

It is an "everyone knows" that study and learning are natural phenomena. Everyone knows that people are born with the ability to learn and the skills of proper study. If that were the case, American high schools would not be graduating droves of "functional illiterates." It has become a national scandal. Obviously, there is something to know about this subject called "study."

If the computer professional is going to become known for his technical expertise, he is going to have to know how to study.

That is "secret skill" number one: the ability to study.

With sufficient technical competence at the professional's command, the next trick is to be able to bring these tools and weapons to bear on the problem at hand in an organized manner. Chapter 5, under the headings of organizing a data structure and writing program specifications, lays out the fundamental skills required to be able to organize, and further reading material is also recommended.

Logical thinking is a skill that everyone knows a computer professional must possess. Logical thinking, however, is merely an extension of the ability to organize. Organizing, as related in chapter  5, rests on first the ability to distinguish similarities, differences and identities and second the ability to discern relative importance. Both these abilities, to distinguish and to discern, depend upon the ability to observe. It is not a high-level ability to observe that is required: simply can one look at a table and determine that it is not a blade of grass. Is one willing to look at a cat and see that it is not a mountain lion. Can one look at a request for a floozle bin report and see the data that will be required to produce that report. Observation requires honesty. Vision clouded by lies is no vision at all.

If a computer professional wants to be absolutely brilliant, logical thinking is the key.

The second "secret skill" is the willingness to honestly observe and organize that which has been seen.

The final secret skill is probably the most important. Without this ability, all your technical expertise, all your study, all your observation and brilliant organization goes out the window. Very simply, one must communicate. Before you wave that off as "well, of course, everyone knows that!" be aware that what is about to follow is probably the simplest daily action anyone could ever take, one simple daily action that can make the difference between a computer wizard and a nerd, one obvious daily action that everyone would think of as almost "required" but very few people do.

Chapter 1 said that virtually all system failures, cost over-runs, late projects, are team failures – failures to communicate. This is true on the large scale (user didn't tell the analyst the requirements, analyst failed to relate the requirements, designer overlooked the program specifications) but also on a day-to-day basis. If communication is maintained on the minor daily scale, most of the team failures mentioned in chapter 1 will be avoided.

The most important "secret skill" is a willingness to communicate.

The simplest and most obvious method of maintaining daily communication is in the hands of the computer professional. At the end of the day, write a brief (one page or less) note describing what was done that day. Address it to whoever you think should be aware of what is happening on the project. For instance, let us say that there was a problem in the Invoicing Program – the address was coming out in the wrong place. Jack, the accountant, is very concerned about it, Jennifer, the computer operator who has to re-type all the invoices, wants the problem solved, and Gene, the credit manager, has asked about it, indicating more than a passing interest. On August 6th, you address the problem and communicate your findings to the users:

```
                  August 6

Jack, Jennifer, Gene:

Addresses on Invoices

The problem was that an old
version of the "address mask"
was being used in the program.
The new, correct, version has
been installed.  The old version
has been erased so this problem
will never recur.  The new
version has been tested on my
test data (see test invoice
attached).

I also checked out the credit
memo program to ensure it was
using the correct mask.  A
slight adjustment was needed
(see test attached).

                  Lucy Chips

                  Computer Wiz
```

The note does not have to be elegant. Good grammar and spelling are desirable, but of paramount importance is that the note tells the people concerned what they need to know.

If trouble is being experienced on a project, the first place it should come up is in conversations with project managers or users, but then it must be memorialized in one of these daily notes.

It is important that these notes include all the things that the user, or project manager, will need to know. It is important that they be concise and *brief*. It is important that they include anything the project manager or users will need to act on. And it is very very important that you admit that you committed an error if you did.

The motto is: tell the truth, the whole truth and nothing but the truth – but you don't have to detail every event of the day either. Only include those things that your reader will have to act on – or no longer needs to act on.

Professional or Flake?

The professional fosters and uses the "secret skills." The nerd, or flake, feels no need to study the user's requirements, to organize the system for the user, or to tell his client what is going on.

The person in the grips of the nerd factor is not interested in completing the project on time and on budget. While on the job, the true professional thinks of nothing else.

The trick is to muster the honesty and courage to be a true professional. The nerd factor can be overcome.

If you are a programmer polishing your professional skills or a company manager hoping to hire one for your business venture, the principles spelled out by John Chambers are the key to success. Or, at least, the key to avoiding some of the most avoidable causes of failure. As a professional programmer and IT director, I can identify with these principles and have seen the consequences of hiring programmers who have not yet learned them. "The Nerd Factor" should be an eye-opening read for anyone wanting to properly guide the programmer's role in a team environment and for private contractors building professional relationships.

Success is when programmers provide what the customer wants. Whether for public use or in-house systems, the people who use our software are our customers. Our first task is to learn from customers what they want, our final task is to ensure they approve of what you have delivered. John Chambers has very neatly laid out the steps to getting there.

Viken Nokhoudian
Phone App Developer
Santa Barbara, California

The parts of [*The Nerd Factor*] I enjoyed the most involve the hidden insights into software development, such as:
- Personality types of individuals that can sink a project
- The user as key to success of a software project
- Software projects evolve

Lindsay Bassett
Software Development Entrepreneur
Grants Pass, Oregon